YOUR ATM

(ABILITY TO MANIFEST)

Neo Positivity

ACKNOWLEDGEMENTS

If anyone claims to be a self made man or woman, it's a shame, because they are simply not seeing the bigger picture. This book, and who I am today, is the result of the people who influenced me, challenged me, and helped shape me along the way.

I have been blessed with so many family members who were influential in shaping who I am today, far too many to list individually in this acknowledgement. Every one of them influenced me in a major way. My siblings and cousins, especially, played a huge role in who I became growing up.

When my children came into my life, they took over in shaping me into the man I am today. They are my greatest joys and my greatest creations, and they continue to push me to live, think, and lead at a higher level. Tatiana, Antonio, and Amor, I love you so much.

The biggest acknowledgement goes to my father, Suso Davila. To this day, he is the greatest man I have ever met. A natural born leader, helper, and giver. I have watched him like a hawk for 44 years now. Everyone he has ever met looks up to him naturally. Whether that gift was taught, inherited, or both, it's played a major role in every success I have experienced in my life. It honestly made things easier by allowing me to be more myself in situations where many people bend to fit in or "stay in their lane". Being myself, exactly as I am and exactly where I am from, is what opened doors into bigger rooms. I was truly blessed to have him as my mentor. I love you, Dad.

To my friends, fans, and supporters, thank you for the messages, conversations, and stories you shared with me. Many times when the views, likes, and shares were scarce, and I felt like the world wasn't listening, I considered giving social media a rest and just using these tools for myself and my family. It was your inboxes and DMs that reminded me of the bigger picture. I was put here to nourish and share this information.

Your stories and gratitude kept me going, kept me pushing, and kept me raging against the machine by sharing this world-changing information they do not want us to know.

Thank you to Elijah Desmond for treating me like a brother from day one, for bringing me into the dental world, putting me on stages, and giving me the space to speak my truth, which exploded my career.

A special thank you to Corey and Jenny Roletto for being the largest financial supporters of this book. Corey is also a thought leader who continually asks how he can help me spread this message.

(Note: A large part of what I receive is donations towards the movement. If you are interested, I would love to have you involved. Simply go to NeoPositivity.com and find out how to make a donation)

And to everyone who supported this book through pre-orders, contributions, and belief in this vision, thank you. Your support helped turn this message into something tangible, and I am deeply grateful.

TABLE OF CONTENTS

CHAPTER ONE:
THOUGHTS BECOME THINGS
(AND YOU'VE BEEN PROVING IT YOUR WHOLE LIFE)

Let me tell you something that's going to change everything.

Your life right now, the house you're in, the car you drive, the job you have, the relationships you're in, the money in your bank account, all of it is the result of your previous thoughts. Every single bit of it. And I'm not talking about some woo-woo hippie stuff. I'm talking about physics. I'm talking about laws that govern this universe the same way gravity does.

You can deny gravity all you want. You can say it doesn't exist. You can tell yourself it doesn't apply to you. But if you jump off a building, you're going to hit the ground. Period. The Law of Attraction works the same way. You've been using it your whole life, you just didn't know it. And because you didn't know it, you've been using it backwards.

Most people fail at manifestation not because the Law of Attraction doesn't work. They fail because they don't realize they're already manifesting 24/7. Every single thought you have is like placing an order with the universe. And the universe doesn't care if that order is for something good or something bad. It just delivers what you focus on the most.

Think about that for a second.

The universe doesn't give a damn if you're thinking about something you want or something you're scared of. It just sees energy. It sees frequency. And it matches that frequency with experiences that vibrate the same way.

This is science. This isn't me making this up.

The Third Law of Motion (And Why You Should Care)

Isaac Newton figured this out centuries ago: every action has an opposite and equal reaction. You throw a ball at a wall, it bounces back. You put good energy out, good energy comes back. You put negative energy out, negative energy comes back.

When you have a thought, it gets dispersed across the entire universe. Then it gets reversed right back at you. And the world will do whatever it has to do for the law of motion to maintain its statute as a law.

Let me say that again because it's important: **When you have a thought, it gets dispersed across the entire universe, then it gets reversed right back at you. Then the world will do whatever it needs to, for the law of motion to maintain its statue.**

That's not philosophy. That's proven physics. And it's as real as gravity itself. Scientists have discovered that physical matter is made of cells. Cells are made of molecules. Molecules are made of atoms. Atoms are made of subatomic particles. And subatomic particles are made of something called quarks. Quarks can only be moved or manipulated by conscious effort. By thoughts. Powered, fueled, and strengthened by emotions.

Read that again. The things that make up everything around you, this book, your phone, your body…can only be moved by conscious effort/thought.

Everything is energy. And that energy responds to your thoughts just like a pebble tossed into water causing waves..

Einstein said it best: "Everything is energy and that's all there is to it. Match the frequency of the reality you want and you cannot help but get that reality. It can be no other way. This is not philosophy. This is physics."

Little Timmy and the Bully

Let me give you an example of how this works in real life.

There's a kid I call Little Timmy. He lives in the hood I grew up in. Every morning when Timmy wakes up, the first thought in his mind is the bully at school who beats on him every day..

So Timmy's thinking about this bully while he's brushing his teeth. He's thinking about him while he's walking to school. He takes a different route just in case the bully's waiting for him somewhere. The whole time, thinking about previous punches received.

He gets to school. And guess what? The bully starts beating on him. And Timmy's standing there thinking, "Why is this happening to me?"

Because he's been thinking about it all day most days.

He expected it to happen. And what you truly expect is what you get.

I grew up in this neighborhood. Camden City, New Jersey. Always the poorest and 6 years in a row the most dangerous city in America. When I went to schools like Mcgraw or Woodrow Wilson High School in, I expected friction. My first day, I knew there'd be problems. And guess what? There were.

But here's the thing, I also expected to handle it. I expected to be okay. And I was.

That expectation shaped everything.

Your thoughts become your reality. The question is: are you going to keep thinking about what you don't want, or are you going to start thinking about what you want?

The Elephant in the Living Room

Now, before you get too excited, let me be clear about something. Obviously, you can't just think about an elephant in your living room and one appears out of thin air. That's not how this works.

The Law of Attraction isn't magic. It's not instant. It's not "think it and it appears."

It's about frequency. It's about vibration. It's about what you focus on most of the time coupled with your expectations.

You have somewhere between 60,000 to 70,000 thoughts per day. That's a lot of thoughts. And the universe is tallying them up. It's like votes in an election. And majority wins.

If 51% of your thoughts today are focused and believing in being broke, struggling, stressed, and worried, guess what your tomorrow is going to look like?

If 51% of your thoughts today are focused and believing in abundance, confidence, gratitude, and success, guess what your tomorrow is going to look like?

It's that simple. And it's that hard.

Because here's the problem: most people don't even realize what they're thinking about most of the day. They're on autopilot. They're running the same mental programs they've been running for years. And those programs are producing the same results they've been getting for years.

If you want different results, you need different thoughts. Period.

How I Found Out About This

I was a cop in Camden City. At the time, it was ranked the most dangerous city in America. I'm talking about a place where I got hurt every single year I was on the force. Broken bones, injuries, fights every night. I was chasing people in cars, and on foot, hourly (most days). It was a war zone. And everyone hated us. Until their house got broken into.

But I was obsessed with the brain. Always have been. Since I was a kid, I wanted to understand how people think, why they do what they do, how the mind works.

My partner at the time told me he was a retired CIA agent. I never looked into it, but he was one of the smartest guys I'd met, so I believed him. One day he tells me there's a book they make all the CIA recruits read at the academy. He said, "You'd really enjoy it. It's called *The Secret*."

Now, I'm a SWAT-type guy. Rapid deployment. Man's man. Cop's cop. So when I went to pick up this movie called The Secret, I'm thinking it's going to be some tactical, SWAT-type thing.

It wasn't.

It was about the Law of Attraction. About how your thoughts shape your reality. About how what you focus on is what you create.

And I'm sitting there watching this movie, and puzzle pieces that have been missing my whole life just started clicking into place. It all made sense, finally.

I Was Already Doing It (And Didn't Even Know It)

Here's what blew my mind: I realized I'd been using the Law of Attraction my entire life without knowing it.

In high school, I was a wide receiver on the football team. We didn't have Friday night games because of the fights, etc. We had Saturday morning games at like 10 a.m. I had to be in the locker room by like 7:30 a.m.

And every week I'd go out to the field early when nobody else was there. No crowd, no noise. Just me and the empty field. And I'd stand there near the goal post and visualize. I didn't know why I was compelled to do this before every game but I didn't question it either.

I'd see myself running a route. Ten yards then out. Catch it. Boom. Quick slant. Catch it. Boom. Post pattern. Catch it. Boom. I'd visualize my offense marching down the field, making play after play, all the way to the end zone. Then I'd start over.

I'd do this over and over. And every now and then, one of my teammates would come outside and say, "Yo Neomaya, you good? (They all knew me by my complete name) What are you doing out here?"

And I'd say, "Just going over the playbook."

To them, I was just standing there staring at grass. But in my mind, I was running plays. I was feeling the ball in my hands. I was there.

I never knew why I did that. I just felt like I had to.

When I saw The Secret, I realized what I'd been doing all along. I was visualizing. I was proactively manifesting. I was training my brain to expect success.

And it worked.

"The Secret" Changed Everything

March 11, 2008. That's the day I first watched The Secret. I'll never forget it.

By November 28, 2008, I was retired. Full pension. Untaxed. At 28 years old.

Just eight months.

There were plenty of ups and downs, eating chili and white rice with my kids three to four nights a week because that's all I could afford. But in the end, I was retired living the good life.

And I'll tell you the full story later in this book. But right now, I need you to understand something:

I didn't get lucky. I didn't win the lottery. I didn't inherit money.

I changed my thoughts. And my thoughts changed my life.

Your Life Is the Result of Your Previous Thoughts

Look around you right now. I mean it, actually look around.

Your house. Your car. Your job. Your relationship status. Your bank account. Your health.

All of it, all of it, is the result of your previous thoughts.

And I know what you're thinking right now. You're thinking, "Neo, I didn't think about getting hurt. I didn't think about being broke. I didn't think about my relationship falling apart."

Yes, you did.

You just didn't realize it.

You worried about getting hurt. You stressed about money. You focused on what wasn't working in your relationship.

And the universe said, "Okay, here's more of that."

Because the universe doesn't distinguish between what you want and what you don't want. It only registers what you're focusing on.

If you're focused on debt, you get more debt. If you're focused on sickness, you get more sickness. If you're focused on drama, you get more drama.

But if you're focused on abundance, you get more abundance. If you're focused on health, you get more health. If you're focused on peace, you get more peace.

It's not magic. It's science. And you've been proving it your whole life.

The question is: are you ready to use it purposefully? Honing your skills like a sniper.

The Finger-Rub Wake-Up

Here's your first mental exercise. And I'm going to give you a lot of these throughout this book. Some will be simple. Some will be more complex. But this one? This one compliments the foundation of everything.

I want you to rub your index finger and middle finger against your thumb. Like you're making the money gesture. You know what I'm talking about.

Do it right now.

Feel that? That texture. That friction. That's real. That's happening right now.

When you do that, you automatically snap back to this moment. You disassociate from everything else going on in your life, the bills, the stress, the drama, the future, the past, and you come back to now.

And now is the only place where you have any power.

I want you to do this throughout the day. Set a reminder on your phone if you have to. Do it at least ten times today.

Why? Because the hardest part of all of this, and I'll say this a hundred times in this book, is remembering to remember to wake up and do these exercises. Life comes at you fast. Next thing you know, it's bedtime and you haven't done a single mental exercise all day.

So start here. Start with waking up more often every day.

Rub your fingers together. Feel it. Say to yourself, "I'm here. I'm present. This is now."

That's it. That's the exercise.

Simple? Yes. Powerful? You have no idea.

You've been manifesting your whole life. The only difference now is that you know it. And what you do with that knowledge is going to determine everything that happens next.

Welcome to the game. Let's play it right this time.

CHAPTER TWO:
YOUR BRAIN: THE ORGAN THAT BEHAVES
LIKE A MUSCLE

Your brain is a muscle.

Not literally, I'm not saying it's made of the same tissue as your biceps or your quads. But it functions like one. And just like any other muscle in your body, it gets stronger at whatever it does, or you make it do, repeatedly.

If you go to the gym and do bicep curls every day, your biceps get bigger. If you run every day, your legs get stronger. If you practice piano every day, your fingers learn the movements without you thinking about them.

Your brain works the exact same way.

Whatever you think about most, your brain gets better at thinking about. Whatever you focus on repeatedly becomes automatic. It becomes muscle memory.

And here's the problem: most people have been training their brains to think negatively for years. . They've been lifting the wrong weights. And they wonder why their life looks the way it does. Self preservation is a main contributor to negative thought patterns and beliefs.

Neural Pathways and Mental Muscle Memory

There's a concept in neuroscience called neural pathways. Think of them like trails in the woods.

The first time you walk through the woods, there's no path. You're pushing through bushes, stepping over logs, breaking branches. It's hard work.

But if you walk that same route every single day, eventually a path forms. The grass gets worn down. The dirt gets packed. And now it's easy to walk that path. You don't even have to think about it anymore. Your feet just know where to go.

That's what happens in your brain.

Every time you have a thought, you're creating or reinforcing a neural pathway. The more you think that thought, the stronger that pathway becomes. The stronger it becomes, the easier it is for your brain to go down that path again.

And eventually? You don't even have to try to think that thought anymore. Your brain just goes there automatically.

This is why negative thinking is so hard to break. You've been walking down that negative path for years. Maybe decades. Your brain has worn a deep groove into that trail, and now it defaults to that route without you even realizing it.

But here's the good news: you can create new paths. You can train your brain to think differently. You just have to be intentional about it. And work on it daily. This isn't like a black belt, where once you have it it's yours forever. It's more like jogging. You have to consistently work at it to be good at it.

The Facebook Algorithm (But for Your Brain)

Let me give you an analogy that'll make this crystal clear.

Do you ever notice how Facebook knows exactly what to show you? You watch one cat video, and suddenly your whole feed is cats. You click on one political post, and now you're drowning in political content.

That's not an accident. That's the algorithm.

Facebook's algorithm is designed to show you more of what you engage with. It learns what you like, what you click on, what you spend time looking at. And then it gives you more of that.

Your brain works the exact same way.

If you spend all day thinking about problems, your brain says, "Oh, you like problems? Here are more problems to think about." If you spend all day worrying about money, your brain says, "Oh, you're focused on lack? Let me show you everything you don't have." If you spend all day thinking about what's wrong with your spouse, your brain says, "Oh, you want to focus on their flaws? Here are 47 more things they do that annoy you." Your brain is constantly filtering reality to match what you've been focusing on.

And the scariest part? You don't even realize it's happening. Because it's automatic.

60,000 to 70,000 Thoughts Per Day

You have somewhere between 60,000 to 70,000 thoughts per day.
Let that sink in for a second.
Sixty to seventy thousand thoughts. Every single day.
And here's the kicker: scientists estimate that 94% or more of those thoughts are on autopilot. You're not consciously choosing them. They're just running in the background like programs on your computer.

In my speeches, I tell people to imagine their brain as a computer. You've got all these programs running in the background; some you installed on purpose, some got installed without you knowing, and some have been running so long you forgot they were even there.

And those programs are running your life.

If 94% of your thoughts are on autopilot, that means you're only consciously controlling about 6% of what's going on in your head. Six percent. That's it. The other 94% is just replaying old patterns, old fears, old beliefs, old conditioning. And that's what's creating your reality. So if you want to change your life, you've got to change the autopilot. You've got to reprogram the algorithm. You've got to train your brain to default to better thoughts. And the only way to do that is through repetition.

How I Lost 69 Pounds Without Exercise

Let me tell you something that proves this works. I used to weigh 264 pounds. Now I'm 195. That's 69 pounds lost.

And I didn't exercise. Not once. The injuries I sustained as a cop, both ankles, both knees, both wrists, both shoulders, my spine, working out wasn't an option for me.

You know what I did instead? I changed what I was thinking about food. I ate at least one cheeseburger or cheesesteak every single day while losing the weight. And I did it all publicly on Facebook so people could watch in real time.

Because I understood something most people don't: there is no food, no molecule, nothing on this Earth that can make a person fat, except the belief that what they're eating is making them fat. If you believe the food is making you fat, it's going to make you fat. If you believe your body knows how to process it, if you believe you're healthy and strong regardless of what you eat, that's what happens.

I created mental exercises around that concept, mirror work, affirmations while eating, mental reframes about what food actually does. Every single day, multiple times a day, I'd do these exercises and eat my cheeseburger. And the weight came off. Week after week. The world watched on Facebook. That's what gained me my first big following.

My ego fought me at first. Because logic says you can't eat cheeseburgers every day and lose weight. But I wasn't operating on logic. I was operating on belief. And belief is stronger than logic every single time.

Years later, after I'd already lost the weight, I learned about dendrites and how your brain creates associations. That's when I trained myself to drive past my favorite cheesesteak spot without even a craving. Just neutral. Like it wasn't even there. (We'll get into exactly how I did all of this in later chapters, the specific exercises, the techniques, how you can do it too.)

But first, I had to prove to myself that belief was more powerful than the food itself. And once I proved that, everything else became easy.

Dendrites and the Hot Dog Story

Here's another example of how your brain creates associations without you even realizing it.

There's this thing in your brain called dendrites. They're like little arms that reach out from your neurons (your brain cells) and connect thoughts, memories, and experiences together.

Here's the science. When you have an experience, your brain fires electrical signals. And when two things happen at the same time, those electrical signals create a magnetic pull. The dendrites literally reach out and connect those two experiences. Scientists have a phrase for it: "Neurons that fire together, wire together."

Let's say you're eating a hot dog. You're enjoying it. Just as you're about to take a bite, you hear a car accident behind you. You turn and look, fender bender, everyone's ok. So you continue eating. A year later you don't eat hot dogs anymore and here's why:

Now, your brain has linked "hot dog" with "car accident." The dendrites connected those two experiences because they happened at the same time. And from that moment on, every time you think about hot dogs, your brain might bring up anxiety, fear, or just a general bad feeling. You might not even remember why you don't like hot dogs anymore. You just... don't.

That's your dendrites at work. That's the electrical process happening in your brain every single day, creating associations you never asked for. So ask yourself, what other connections have been made over the years that you're unaware of?

But here's the good news. If your brain can create negative associations automatically, you can create positive associations intentionally. You can train your dendrites to link success with your name. To link confidence with your actions. To link abundance with your future.

To link health with the food you eat. It's the same process. Same neurons. Same electrical signals. Same dendrites reaching out and connecting. You're just doing it on purpose this time.

That's what I did with food. I intentionally fired the neurons for "cheeseburger" at the same time I fired the neurons for "healthy" and "strong" and "energized." And I did it over and over until those dendrites wired together. And once they did, my brain stopped associating cheeseburgers with getting fat. It started associating them with fuel.

That's not magic. That's neuroscience. That's your brain doing what it's designed to do. And you can use this to your advantage. You just have to be intentional. You have to repeat the associations you want until the dendrites connect. Until the new pathway is stronger than the old one.

Because your brain is always making connections. The question is: are you letting it make them randomly? Or are you creating the connections that serve your goals?

Change the Algorithm, Change Your Life

So here's the truth: if you want a different life, you need different thoughts. Not just once. Not just when you feel like it. Not just when things are going well. You need to change your default thoughts. You need to reprogram the autopilot. And that takes work, discipline, repetition, time, and dedication. But it's worth it. Because once you change the algorithm, everything else changes with it.

Your brain will start showing you opportunities instead of obstacles. Solutions instead of problems. Abundance instead of lack. Not because the world changed. Because you changed. And your brain is now filtering reality through a different lens.

Mental Check-Ins

Here's your second mental exercise, and this one's going to be a habit you build over time.

Three times a day, morning, afternoon, and night, I want you to stop and ask yourself this question:

"Have my thoughts been serving me today?"

That's it. Just ask the question. Don't beat yourself up if the answer is no. The thoughts you had were the exact ones you were meant to have. Move forward.

Awareness is the first step to change. You can't change what you're not aware of. And most people go through their entire lives never once stopping to ask, "Wait, what have I been thinking about all day?"

So start noticing. Start checking in.

Morning: "Have my thoughts been serving me today?"

Afternoon: "Have my thoughts been serving me today?"

Night: "Have my thoughts been serving me today?"

That's it. Simple. Powerful.

And over time, you'll start catching yourself in negative thought patterns before they spiral. You'll start redirecting your thoughts before they create problems. Because your brain is like a muscle. And you're about to start training it the right way.

Stay Insane or Change

There's a saying that gets thrown around a lot: "The definition of insanity is doing the same thing over and over again and expecting different results." You've probably heard it. Maybe even said it yourself. Well, guess what? If you keep thinking the same thoughts over and over again and expecting your life to change, that's insanity too.

You can't keep replaying the same mental programs and expect a different outcome. You can't keep worrying about the same things, stressing about the same things, complaining about the same things, and think your life is somehow going to magically improve.

It won't.

You've got to change the input if you want different output. And that starts with your thoughts. With your neural pathways. With your brain algorithm. So the question is: are you going to stay insane? Or are you going to change? Because change is possible. I've done it. I've seen thousands of other people do it. And you can do it too. But you've got to make the decision. And you've got to commit to the work.

Thought Foundations (The House You're Building)

Here's something most people don't realize. Every thought you have sits on a foundation. Just like a house.

And just like a house, you can paint the walls pretty colors. You can put up nice decorations. You can make it look good on the surface. But if the foundation is built on crap, the house is crap.

Your thoughts work the same way.

You can do all the affirmations you want. You can visualize all day long. You can say "I'm wealthy, I'm confident, I'm successful" a thousand times. But if the foundation those thoughts are sitting on is made of doubt, fear, and limiting beliefs, those pretty affirmations aren't going to hold up.

Let me explain what I mean. Self-preservation is a foundational component of every single thought you have. It's running in the background 24/7. And self-preservation, by its very nature, is negative. It's always preparing for the worst. It's always scanning for danger. It's always asking, "What could go wrong?"

So even when you're not consciously thinking about debt, failure, or worst-case scenarios, those thought foundations are still there. Still active. Still influencing every decision you make, every action you take, every outcome you create.

And here's the problem. Over 94% of your thoughts are on autopilot. Which means over 94% of your thoughts are being built on foundations you didn't consciously choose. Foundations that were installed when you were a kid. Foundations based on your parents' beliefs about money, success, relationships, and life. Foundations shaped by trauma, rejection, failure, and fear.

And if thoughts become things, and 94% of your thoughts are on autopilot, then your future is being created based on old programming. Programming that has the foundational component of whatever your subconscious believes to be true about you, about life, about what's possible.

That's why someone can do affirmations every day and still not see results. Because they're trying to build a mansion on a foundation made of sand. And it doesn't matter how pretty the mansion looks. If the foundation is weak, it's going to crumble.

So here's the rule you need to accept. And this is one of the most important rules in this book. Keeping track of and maintaining, and yes, altering, your thought foundations should be a top priority.

Not just your thoughts. Your thought foundations. The beliefs those thoughts are sitting on. The assumptions. The fears. The doubts. The old programming that's been running for years without you even realizing it.

Because if you don't work on the foundation, nothing else you do is going to stick. You'll manifest something for a little while, and then you'll lose it. You'll make progress, and then you'll slide back. You'll feel good for a few days, and then you'll crash. Because the foundation wasn't strong enough to support the life you're trying to build.

And here's the hardest part. Most people know their thought foundations need work. They know they've got limiting beliefs. They know they've got fears and doubts buried deep in their subconscious. But they don't prioritize fixing them.

It's like signing up for a gym membership because you know your health is important. And then only going the first two days and never going again. Because your health is important, sure. But it's not as important to you as other things. Like surfing the internet. Like watching TV. Like staying comfortable.

The same thing happens with thought foundations. You know they're important. You know they need work. But unless you make them a priority, unless you actually do the mental exercises, set the alarms, track your thoughts, reprogram the autopilot, nothing's going to change.

That brain algorithm will never get altered. You'll keep having the same foundational thoughts. Which means you'll keep creating the same outcomes you're currently having. Which is the opposite reason you're reading this book.

So make this a priority. Work on your thought foundations daily. Because every time you water a seed, every time you do an affirmation, every time you visualize your future, you're either building on a strong foundation or trying to stack bricks on quicksand.

And you can't build the life you want on quicksand.

In order for change you must change, but you gotta know how, knowledge is not only power, it's the key. What have you been focusing on? Between proactively thinking, Life's a garden and you've been watering seeds.

And when they bloom, don't be surprised if what's in front of your eyes is the same thing you see daily or worse.

Negativity breeds negative outcomes, positivity thoughts breed positive outcomes, "thoughts become things" can be a gift or a curse.

-From "The Resume"

You've been training your brain your whole life. The only question now is: what are you training it for?

CHAPTER THREE: WATERING SEEDS (WHAT YOU'RE GROWING WITHOUT EVEN KNOWING)

Life is a garden. And you've been watering seeds.

The problem is, most people have no idea which seeds they're watering. They're just walking around with a watering can, pouring water everywhere, and then wondering why weeds keep growing in their life.

Let me explain.

Every thought you have is a drop of water. And in front of you, right now, whether you see them or not, are infinite flower pots. Each one represents something in your life:

- There's a pot labeled "Things I Like About My Job."
- There's a pot labeled "Things I Hate About My Job."
- There's a pot labeled "Why My Spouse Is Amazing."
- There's a pot labeled "Everything My Spouse Does Wrong."
- There's a pot labeled "Reasons I'm Going to Succeed."
- There's a pot labeled "Reasons I'm Going to Fail."
- There's a pot labeled "I'm Healthy and Strong."
- There's a pot labeled "I'm Sick and Tired."

Every single thought you have (65,000 on average per day per person) is a drop of water going into one of those pots.

And whichever pot gets the most water? That's the one that's going to bloom.

The Flower Pot You're Watering Most

Here's the truth nobody wants to hear: you're already manifesting. Right now. Today. This very second. So many people I talk to say that they love the concept but they're going to start next week. That's not how it works.

The question isn't "Does the Law of Attraction work?" The question is "Which pot are you watering?" Because the universe doesn't care if you're watering the "success" pot or the "failure" pot. It just delivers whatever you're focused on most and what you believe the most.

Majority Rules

Majority rules. Always.

If most of your time and energy, your emotion, is spent thinking about how broke you are, how you can't afford things, how bills are piling up, and you truly believe that's your reality, guess what's going to keep showing up in your life? More situations that make you feel broke.

If most of your time and energy is spent thinking about drama, problems, what's going wrong, and you truly believe life is hard, guess what you're going to keep experiencing? More drama. More problems. More reasons to believe life is hard.

But if most of your time and energy is spent thinking about abundance, gratitude, solutions, opportunities, and you truly believe good things are coming, guess what starts showing up? More abundance. More opportunities. More reasons to be grateful.

It's not about hitting "greater than or equal to 51% positive today." It's about where the majority of your focus goes. It's about what you truly believe is going to happen. Because the universe delivers whatever you're emotionally invested in most. Whatever feeling you're spending the most time in, that's the feeling you're going to manifest in your life, by whatever incident necessary.

The universe is counting your thoughts and emotions like votes in an election. And whichever side gets the most votes wins. And it will bring that emotion to you again (3rd law of motion) via any situation it deems necessary.

What have you been voting for? Look around you.

So the real question is: What are you going to do to influence your next vote?

The Coins on the Table

In my seminars, I use a different analogy to explain this, and people tell me it's the one that finally made it click for them.

Imagine a table covered in coins laid flat (none on top of each other). The coin in the center represents you. Now, at the edge of the table, far away from you, there's another coin. That coin represents something you want. A new job. A relationship. Financial freedom. A healthier body. Whatever it is, that's the coin.

We Are Tuning Forks

Here's how it works: when you think about that thing you want, you start vibrating at the same frequency as that outer coin. Any two things that vibrate at the same frequency naturally pull towards each other so that coin starts moving toward you.

But here's the thing: it doesn't just move by itself. As it moves, it shifts dozens of other coins around it. Even by the slightest millimeter, it's moving other coins. Bumping them. Nudging them.

And those other coins? Those represent people. People having conversations about you. People thinking about hiring you. People considering reaching out to you. People presenting you with opportunities. That's how manifestation works. You're not just pulling one thing toward you. You're shifting the entire universe to align with your desires.

But, and this is critical, the second you stop thinking about it, that coin stops moving toward you.

Worse than that? It starts moving away from you.

Because your current situation is proof to your brain of the way things are. And when you're not actively thinking about your goal, you default back to your current reality. You start thinking about your current house, your current job, your current bank account. And that vibration, that frequency of where you are right now, is the opposite of where you're trying to go.

So that outer coin, that goal you were pulling toward you, it doesn't just stop. It reverses. It moves away from you. Because you're no longer vibrating at the frequency that matches it. You're vibrating at the frequency of your current circumstances. And the universe delivers what you're focused on most.

That's why consistency matters. That's why you can't just visualize once and forget about it. You have to keep thinking about it. Keep feeling it. Keep vibrating at that frequency. Because the moment you stop, the coin starts drifting back to where it was.

The Billionaire Coin

Let's say you're trying to manifest being a billionaire. That's your outer coin. And you're sitting in the middle of the table as your current self, maybe making $50,000 a year, living paycheck to paycheck, struggling with bills.

When you focus on being a billionaire, that coin starts moving toward you. Slowly. But it's moving. But then you stop. You get distracted. You go to work. You check your bank account and see $127. You stress about rent. You worry about your car payment. Now, what are you doing? You're vibrating at the frequency of your current reality. And your current reality is far from being a billionaire. So that billionaire coin? It stops. And it starts moving away from you.

Because billionaire energy and broke energy are on opposite ends of the spectrum. They can't exist in the same space. This is why manifestation feels so hard for most people. They focus on what they want for five minutes. Then they spend the rest of the day focused on what they don't have. And the universe says, "Okay, I'm confused. Which one do you actually want? Because you keep changing your vote."

You've got to be consistent. You've got to stay focused. You've got to keep watering the right seed.

The Next Best Shot

Here's something most people get wrong about manifestation. They try to go from broke to billionaire in one jump. From single to soulmate overnight. From entry-level to CEO by next month.

And their ego laughs at them. Because that's too big of a leap. The gap between where you are and where you're trying to go is so massive that your subconscious just can't believe it. And without belief, there's no manifestation.

So instead of shooting for the stars immediately, focus on your next best shot. Not the ultimate goal. The next milestone.

If you're trying to manifest a million dollars and you currently have $5,000 in the bank, don't focus on the million. Focus on getting to $10,000. Then $25,000. Then $50,000. Each time you hit a milestone, your confidence in your ATM, your Ability To Manifest, gets stronger. And that confidence makes the next milestone more believable.

It's like Will Smith talks about when he was a kid building a brick wall with his father. His dad told him, "Don't worry about the wall. Just lay this brick as perfectly as a brick can be laid." And he laid one brick. Then another. Then another. And eventually, he had a wall.

Or Jerry Rice, arguably the greatest wide receiver of all time. His brother used to stand on the ground and throw bricks up to the second floor where Jerry was helping their dad with construction. Jerry's only job? Catch the next brick. Not all the bricks. Just the next one. Then the next one. Then the next one. That focus, that presence, trained him to be unstoppable.

That's how manifestation works. You don't manifest the whole wall. You manifest the next brick. And each brick you successfully lay builds your confidence that you can lay the next one.

This keeps you present. It keeps your ego from freaking out. And it keeps you focused on what's actually achievable right now, which creates momentum instead of resistance.

Energy Dollars

Here's another way to think about it.

You have approximately 65,000 thoughts per day. Let's call each thought an Energy Dollar. That means you have $65,000 to spend every single day.

The universe is watching where you spend it.

If you spend $40,000 of those thoughts on stress, worry, fear, and doubt, and only $25,000 on confidence, gratitude, and abundance, guess which one the universe delivers?

Stress. Worry. Fear. Doubt.

Because you spent more money there. The universe doesn't judge your purchases. It just delivers what you bought the most of. So at the end of each day, ask yourself: "Where did I spend my Energy Dollars today?" Did you spend them on the life you want? Or the life you're trying to escape?

"I'll Start Monday"

I've heard this more than anything else. "I love it Neo, I think I'm going to start on Monday."

You're watering seeds right now. Not Monday. Right now.

Every thought you're having today is a drop of water into a pot. You don't get to pause the universe and say, "Hold on, I'm not ready to manifest yet. Let me get my life together first, then I'll start." No. The universe is paying attention now. The seeds are being watered now. The coins are moving now.

So if you're sitting there thinking, "I'll start Monday," you're watering the "I'll start Monday" seed. And guess what? Monday comes, and you say it again. "I'll start Monday." That's the seed that keeps blooming. Procrastination. Delay. Excuses. You want to manifest a different life? Start watering different seeds today. Not Monday. Today.

The Seeds You Don't Even Know You're Watering

Here's where it gets tricky.

Most people aren't even aware of which seeds they're watering. They think they're thinking positive. They think they're focused on what they want. 80% of the people I talk to deny having negative thoughts at all. I usually just remind them of a little thing called "self-preservation."

But if you actually tracked their thoughts for a day, you'd see the truth. They say they want financial freedom. But they spend all day thinking about bills, debt, expenses, what they can't afford. They say they want a loving relationship. But they spend all day thinking about what their partner doesn't do, what they wish was different, arguments from last week. They say they want success. But they spend all day thinking about obstacles, setbacks, people who doubted them, reasons it might not work out.

You can't say you want one thing and then spend your Energy Dollars on the opposite. It doesn't work that way. The universe doesn't listen to your words. It listens to your focus. It listens to where your attention goes. It listens to which seed you're watering most. And if you're watering the wrong seed, don't be surprised when that's the one that blooms.

Watering Seeds Audit

Here's your mental exercise for this chapter, and this one's going to require some honesty. I want you to identify three flower pots you're watering most in your life right now. Not the three you wish you were watering. The three you're actually watering.

Maybe it's:
- "Things I'm worried about"
- "Reasons I'm not good enough"
- "Why life is hard"

Or maybe it's:
- "Things I'm grateful for"
- "Opportunities coming my way"
- "Reasons I'm going to win"

Write them down. Be honest. Don't lie to yourself.

Because you can't change what you're not aware of.

Once you know which pots you're watering, you can make a conscious decision to redirect your focus. To spend your Energy Dollars differently. To water the seeds you actually want to bloom.

Energy Dollars Tracking

Here's the second part of this exercise. At the end of today, before you go to bed, I want you to ask yourself:

"Where did I spend my 65,000 Energy Dollars today?"

Did you spend them on fear? On doubt? On worry? On stress? Or did you spend them on confidence? On gratitude? On possibility? On abundance?

You don't have to be perfect. Nobody is. But you do need to be aware. Because awareness is the first step to change. And once you start tracking where your Energy Dollars are going, you'll start spending them more wisely. You'll catch yourself mid-negative-thought and say, "Wait, I don't want to spend my money on that. Let me redirect." And over time, you'll train your brain to default to the right pots. The right seeds. The right coins. And that's when everything changes.

Majority Rules (Revisited)

Let me say it one more time, because this is the most important thing in this chapter:

Majority rules.

But here's what that really means. It's not just about counting positive versus negative thoughts. It's about what you truly expect deep down inside your subconscious. And here's the problem: you can't directly access your subconscious. It's running programs in the background that you're not even aware of. Programs installed years ago. Programs shaped by your childhood, your experiences, your traumas, your wins, your losses.

Your conscious mind might say, "I want abundance." But if your subconscious believes you don't deserve it, or you're not capable of it, or people like you don't get rich, guess which one wins? The subconscious. Every single time.

That's why affirmations alone don't work for most people. They're trying to override decades of subconscious programming with a few positive statements. And the subconscious just laughs and goes back to running the old program.

So when I say majority rules, I'm talking about two things: what you expect to happen, and your confidence in your ability to manifest it.

You don't have to be positive 100% of the time. That's not realistic. You're human. You're going to have bad days. Negative thoughts are going to pop up. That's normal.

But if the majority of your energy, your emotion, your focus, your belief, is spent expecting good things and trusting in your ability to create them, you're going to manifest good things. Even if you have negative thoughts sprinkled throughout your day.

It's not about perfection. It's about where your subconscious default sits. It's about what you expect when you're not actively trying to control your thoughts. It's about your confidence in your ATM, your Ability To Manifest, being stronger than your doubt.

And you build that confidence one win at a time. One next shot at a time. When you hit your next milestone, even if it's small, you prove to yourself that your ATM works. And that proof makes the next milestone easier to believe in. It's progression. It's the difference between possible, probable, and inevitable. First, something becomes possible, you can see a path. Then it becomes probable, based on your track record, it's likely to happen. Then it becomes inevitable, it's just a matter of time. But you can't skip steps. You have to build the confidence brick by brick.

And once you get to the point where your subconscious expectation is aligned with what you consciously want? That's when miracles start happening.

That's when things you thought were impossible start showing up in your life.

That's when people start asking you, "How did you do that? What's your secret?"

And the secret is simple: you reprogrammed your subconscious. You built confidence in your ability to manifest. You watered the right seeds until the new garden grew stronger than the old one.

What have you been focusing on? Between proactively thinking, Life's a garden and you've been watering seeds. And when they bloom, don't be surprised if what's in front of your eyes is the same thing you see daily or worse. Negativity breeds negative outcomes, positivity thoughts breed positive outcomes,"thoughts become things" can be a gift or a curse.

-From "The Resume"

Life is a garden. You're holding the watering can. The question is: Which seeds are you going to water today?

CHAPTER FOUR:
NO MATTER WHAT YOU ASK FOR,
YOU'LL BE SHOWN YOU CAN'T HAVE IT

No matter what you ask for in life, you will be shown, if not proven, that you cannot have it. And it's how you react to that, that determines if or when you get it.

-Neo

Here's something nobody tells you about manifestation:

No matter what you ask for, the universe is going to test you. It's going to slam doors in your face. It's going to tell you "no" sometimes, repeatedly. It's going to make you feel like you're doing everything wrong.

And most people, when they hit that resistance, quit.

They think, "Well, I guess the Law of Attraction doesn't work for me. I guess I'm not meant to have this. I guess the universe is telling me to give up." Wrong. The universe isn't telling you to give up. It's testing you. It's asking one simple question: "How bad do you want it?" And how you respond to that question, emotionally, mentally, spiritually, determines whether you get what you want or not and when you'll get it.

To Whom Much Is Given, Much Is Tested

There's a biblical principle that says, "To whom much is given, much is required."

I'm going to twist that a little bit for manifestation purposes:

To whom much is given, much is tested.

Before the universe hands you something big, something life-changing, it's going to make sure you can handle it. It's going to make sure you're ready for it.

And the way it does that? By testing your resolve. By seeing if you're going to fold the first time things don't go your way. Think about it. If you can't handle a few rejections, a few closed doors, a few "no's", how are you going to handle the responsibility that comes with getting what you asked for? If you're trying to manifest a million dollars, but you panic every time you lose $100, the universe knows you're not ready for a million.

If you're trying to manifest a relationship, but you spiral every time someone doesn't text you back, the universe knows you're not ready for a healthy partnership. If you're trying to manifest a business, but you quit the first time you get a bad review, the universe knows you're not ready to be a business owner. The test isn't personal. It's practical.

The universe is trying to prepare you for what you're asking for. And if you pass the test, you get the reward. But if you fail, if you give up, complain, run to Facebook to tell everyone your life sucks, the universe says, "Okay, not ready yet. Let's try again later."

The Beautiful Tennis Match

I call this the Beautiful Tennis Match. Here's how it works:

You serve the ball. You say to the universe, "I want this. I deserve this. I'm claiming this."

The universe hits/sends it back. "No, you can't have it."

Ball's in your court. Now, most people, when they get that "no" (could be the 3rd or 4th "no"), they drop the racket and walk off the court. They say, "Well, I tried. Guess it wasn't meant to be." But the people who actually manifest what they want? They hit the ball back. Harder.

"Yes, I can have it. I basically have it already, just in a different timeline. I'm just waiting for the universe to catch up. Watch me." The universe serves it back again. "Nope. Still no."

And you? You hit it back again. "I don't care how many times you say no. I'm not giving up. I got this!"

Back and forth. Back and forth. This beautiful tennis match where you refuse to lose.

And eventually, after the universe sees that you're serious, that you're committed, that you're not going to fold, it stops serving "no" back to you.

It starts serving opportunities (that could come with their own sets of "no's"). Doors start opening. People start showing up. Things start aligning. But you've got to stay in the match. You've got to keep hitting the ball back. Because the second you quit, the game's over.

The Lottery Ticket Story

Let me give you a real-life example from my own life. Back when I first learned about the Law of Attraction, I was broke. Like, eating chili and white rice with my kids three to four nights a week because that's all I could afford. The other nights I'd eat at friends or family's houses.

But I started doing the mental exercises. I started saying affirmations. I started visualizing. And one of the things I told myself every single day was:

"I won the lottery. I won the lottery. I won the lottery."

Now, I wasn't buying lottery tickets every day. I'd buy one here and there. And most of the time? I lost. And every time I lost, my ego would step in and say, "See? You didn't win. Stop lying to yourself." But I kept saying it. "I won the lottery. I won the lottery." And then one day, I won $2. I still have that lottery ticket framed today. Most people would look at that and say, "That's not winning" or "That's just breaking even." But I didn't see it that way. I saw it as proof. Proof that I won. The amount didn't matter. I manifested a win.

So I kept the ticket. I framed it. And I kept saying, "I won the lottery." And you know what happened over the next year? I won 13 times. Not millions. I'm not talking about hitting the jackpot. But I won 13 times in one year. Small amounts. $50 here. $100 there. A few $2 and $5 wins sprinkled in. And every single time, I celebrated like I'd just won a million dollars. Because the universe was teaching me something: I'm a winner.

45

Not because of the money. Because I didn't quit when I lost. I didn't drop the ball. I kept playing the game.

Once again I took Facebook on this journey with me. This new Law of Attraction concept was working and I couldn't keep it to myself. I needed the world to know, and I needed them to see it in real time as it unfolded.

Every Major Manifestation Started With a "No"

Here's the truth: every single major thing I've manifested in my life started with the universe telling me "no."

When I wanted to retire from the police department at 28 with a pension, I was told "no." They stopped paying me illegally, making it as difficult as possible to stay positive. But I didn't quit. I kept doing my mental exercises. And soon after, I retired.

When I wanted to get custody of my kids, the system said no. People told me it was impossible. To this day, I'm the only father I know of who got his kids. New Jersey just doesn't do that. But I didn't accept that. I walked into that courtroom with no lawyer, just the law of attraction and my confidence in my Ability to Manifest, and walked out with everything I asked for.

That's the difference between people who manifest and people who don't. It's not talent. It's not luck. It's persistence.

How You Respond Emotionally Is Everything

Here's what most people don't understand: the universe doesn't care if you encounter obstacles. It cares how you respond to them. Do you panic? Do you complain? Do you give up? Or do you stay calm, stay focused, and keep moving forward?

Because your emotional response is what determines your frequency. And your frequency is what determines what you attract next. If you respond to a "no" with anger, frustration, and defeat, you're vibrating at a low frequency. And guess what you're going to attract more of? More reasons to be angry, frustrated, and defeated.

But if you respond to a "no" with confidence, gratitude, and determination, you're vibrating at a high frequency. And you're going to attract opportunities, solutions, and breakthroughs. The test isn't about whether you face rejection. The test is about whether rejection changes you. And if you let rejection change your energy, you've failed the test.

The Overconfidence Push

Here's a mental exercise that's going to feel uncomfortable at first, but it's one of the most powerful tools I've ever used.

When you're "proactively manifesting" and doing affirmations, go hard with confidence. I want you to push your affirmations to a level that feels almost blasphemous. To a level where your ego is screaming at you to stop. And push further.

Let's say you're trying to make 10 basketball shots in a row and you're on number 5. In your head and heart something in you is going to say "don't get too cocky, or God or the universe will make you miss to humble you". F that! Go harder.

The universe says, "Okay, this one's serious. This one's not going to quit. Let's give them what they're asking for."

Try it!

The Beautiful Tennis Match (Continued)

So here's how the tennis match really works:

You demand. The universe says no. You demand again. The universe says no. You demand again. The universe says no.

And at some point, your friends, your family, even your own mind is going to tell you to give up.

"Maybe it's not meant to be."

"Maybe you're aiming too high."

"Maybe you should just settle."

And that's the moment, right there, where most people quit. But the people who actually manifest? They don't quit. They keep hitting the ball back with more conviction. And that's when the universe says, "Alright. You passed. Here you go."

It's not magic. It's not luck. It's persistence. It's refusing to drop the ball no matter how many times it gets served back to you. And most importantly, it's your confidence in Your ATM… Ability to Manifest.

Never Run to Facebook to Complain

Here's one more thing, and this is critical:

When the universe tests you, when things go wrong, when doors slam, when it feels like nothing's working, do not run to social media to complain about it.

Don't post about how hard life is. Don't vent about how nothing ever works out for you. Don't tell everyone how broke you are or how you're struggling.

Because when you do that, you're inviting hundreds, maybe thousands, of people to send you low-frequency energy. And most of them, out of sympathy, are going to think, "Oh, that's so sad. Poor them. Their life is so hard."

And what are they doing? They're manifesting a bad future for you. Not on purpose. Not with malicious intent. But they're thinking about you in a state of struggle. They're seeing you as someone who's suffering. And that energy, those thoughts, are hitting you whether you realize it or not.

Even people who've never met you. People who only know you're American. Their perception of Americans is a vibration. Your friend from high school who now pities you because of your last few sad posts? That's a vibration hitting your aura.

Floyd Mayweather says it best: whether you pay to see him win or pay to see him lose, either way, you're paying him. And he's not just talking about money. He's talking about energy. Attention is energy. And energy is energy; it doesn't matter if it's good or bad. You can use it however you see fit.

50 Cent said the same thing: "I love my haters. I need them so I can use them for their energy." He understands that whether it's good energy or bad energy, it's still energy coming his way. And he's learned how to transform it.

But most people can't do that. Most people don't know how to take negative energy and turn it into fuel. So when you post your struggles and 1,500 people feel sorry for you, you're getting hit with 1,500 waves of low-frequency energy. And that energy weighs you down. It keeps you stuck in the exact situation you're trying to escape.

So keep your struggles private. Don't broadcast your pain. Don't invite the world to see you as someone who's losing.

Because the energy they send you based on what you show them is the energy that shapes your reality. And if they're all thinking about you struggling, guess what you're going to keep manifesting?

More struggle.

The universe is going to test you. That's a promise. But if you stay in the game, if you keep hitting the ball back, if you refuse to quit, you win. Keep your energy tight/right!

Every single time.

CHAPTER FIVE:
YOUR EGO ISN'T YOUR ENEMY
(IT'S YOUR OVERLY PARANOID BODYGUARD)

So now we need to talk about the elephant in the room. We need to talk about the ego. And this is important because understanding the ego is one of the most critical parts of manifestation. I'm not talking about the kind of ego where someone is arrogant or conceited, thinking they're better than or more important than everyone else. I'm talking about something completely different. Something that's running in the background of each of our minds right now, on autopilot, constantly working, constantly protecting, constantly doing its job, whether we realize it or whether we like it or not.

I first learned about this from a book called *The Power of Now* by Eckhart Tolle. This is the most influential book I've ever read in my life. I saw a YouTube video where someone said that's the book that she sleeps with on her nightstand. As the story goes, she was highlighting so many lines in the first chapter that she just stopped highlighting. Side note: The Power of Now is an amazing book, but Part 2 is called *A New Earth* by Eckhart Tolle, which encompasses everything you'd need to know, IMHO, from Part 1 plus more. So if you're not a big fan of reading, of course use the audiobooks. I live in Florida and everything is half an hour to an hour away, so audiobooks are a great way to get through a book and pass time, making the drive seem to go by faster. Just go ahead and read the second book if you're like me and it would take you months to just get through one of them if you're reading it.

And what I learned from that book changed everything. Because once I learned its purpose, I stopped fighting it. I stopped hating it. And I started working with it instead of against it. Working along with myself for better results as opposed to having an internal struggle.

Let me give you an example of how the ego shows up in your life. I was the best man at my best friend's wedding. I was standing in front of a mirror getting ready, dressed up in my suit. I looked at myself in the mirror and thought, "Man, I clean up good." Immediately there was a little voice that said, "Well, what about that blemish on your face? And you could be five pounds lighter." That's the egoic voice. And it's triggered by anything that isn't aligned with this present moment. Whether I'm telling an accurate statement or not, the ego is going to have an opposing opinion because it just wants to bring me back to this moment.

That moment really brought to light and opened my eyes to recognizing that voice. And recognizing that voice is what led me to start doing mirror exercises, which eventually led to me losing all that weight. I went from 264 pounds down to 195 using what I call The All Mental Diet. No exercise. Just reprogramming my thoughts about food, about my body, and about what I deserved. And every time I stood in front of that mirror, I had to battle that voice. The voice that said I couldn't do it. The voice that reminded me of every failed diet, not only that I've done but that I've heard people fail at. All of that adds up in our minds as proof that diets don't work. The voice that pulled up every piece of evidence that I was lying to myself.

But once I understood what that voice was and why it was there, I stopped letting it influence me so much. I stopped letting it influence my decisions, my moods, which means it was no longer influencing my confidence, which means it was no longer influencing my outcomes, which means it was no longer influencing my life, at least not even a fraction of what it was. Because make no mistake, I didn't, and I don't think you ever can fully get rid of this voice. And we'll talk about that again in a second.

Here's what I mean. If I were to stand in my living room right now and say, "There's a million dollars in cash sitting on the floor right in front of me," and there actually wasn't a million dollars there, my ego would do whatever it had to do to bring me back to this moment of truth, which is that the money's not actually there. It'll prove to me that it's not there by using my subconscious, which stores everything I've ever seen or heard about, or experienced, everything I've ever learned or known, every conclusion I've ever drawn or heard about being drawn. The ego accesses that data bank and uses it to yank me back to this moment.

So anytime I reminisce about a future scenario or think about a moment from the past, the ego just wants me in this moment. If I'm thinking about a future where I'm on a cruise spending unlimited money, the ego says, "You're not on a cruise. You know what it takes to be on a cruise right now. You don't have unlimited money." And it'll throw whatever scenarios it has to at me to prove that what I'm imagining isn't real, just to bring me back to this moment. The same thing happens if I'm thinking about a car accident from ten years ago. The ego might quickly pull me back and say, "That's not happening right now." And it zaps me back to this moment.

Why does it always bring me back to this moment? Because the subconscious and the ego don't acknowledge the future or the past. And that was one of the biggest points I got from The Power of Now by Eckhart Tolle. This is what I learned that changed my life forever.

When trying to get someone to understand what time really is, this is how I demonstrate it in my seminars. I'll ask the crowd: Have you ever seen, touched, or tasted anything from your future? When you experienced that so-called future, you experienced it in the current moment. And as far as the past goes, you can never go back and relive a moment for the first time. You can duplicate it a second time, but you will never be able to go back and experience it again for the first time. So the future and the past literally don't exist. They're just words used to describe experiences either had or possible future experiences. Everything you've ever done and everything you ever will do, you will do in this seemingly recurring current moment.

And that's why the ego will shut down thoughts of the past or the future, because they don't exist, and the ego is constantly trying to bring you back to this moment. It's a form of self-preservation. So when you try to imagine yourself doing something great, living an amazing life, being successful, wealthy, happy, it's not in this moment. It's not true right now. So the ego will use its access to your entire subconscious data bank to wake you up and bring you back to this current moment.

Why does it want you in this moment? Have you ever heard the phrase, "If you want to make God laugh, tell him your plans"? Because His plan is so much bigger than yours. And what I've deciphered from this over the years, using everything I've learned about thoughts becoming things and the Law of Attraction, is this: when you're thinking about the future, you're vibrating at a frequency that's pulling that future toward you. Thus, thoughts become things. Any two things that vibrate at the same frequency will naturally pull toward each other.

As humans, we change our vibrational frequency according to how we're feeling. Because it's the feeling that determines the vibrational frequency. If you were to measure our vibrational frequency on a spectrometer or similar scientific instrument, you'd see it shift based on our emotional state. And any two things that vibrate at the same frequency will naturally pull toward each other. That's the concept I explained with the coins on the table in Chapter 3. When you vibrate at the same frequency as what you want, it moves toward you. But the second you stop thinking about it and start thinking about your current reality instead, that coin stops moving toward you and starts moving away.

That's why the mental exercises in this book are so critical. Over 94% of your thoughts run on autopilot, repeating the same patterns over and over without your conscious input. These exercises snap you out of autopilot. They keep you vibrating at the correct frequency, closer towards your desired future and outcomes, instead of defaulting back to manifesting the same reality you're used to. These mental exercises aren't optional. They're the difference between staying stuck and actually creating change.

But here's what you need to understand: the ego is just doing its job. It's a self-preservation mechanism trying to keep you safe by keeping you in this moment. People hate their ego because it won't allow them to sit in a mindset of "I'm a billionaire" before it shuts you down and says, "No, you're not. No, you won't. What are the chances that'll happen for you?" But it's doing this for you, not to you. It's just programmed to protect you. And to hate a part of you is to manifest more hating a part of you. That's not what we want.

As a police officer, that egoic mindset and self-preservation is what kept me alive. It's what kept me paranoid, which is what kept me disciplined in my training and my experiences, which is what kept me alive in those streets. I was running around chasing bad guys down dark alleyways in the middle of the night in what was the most dangerous city in America, six out of my eight years there, Camden City, New Jersey. So hating that part of you doesn't serve you at all. The ego isn't your enemy. It's your overly paranoid bodyguard. It thinks it's protecting you. And in a lot of ways, it is. You just have to learn how to work with it instead of letting it dictate your decisions, control your outcomes, and run your life.

And here's something critical that I learned from both The Power of Now and The Untethered Soul: that voice is not you. You are the listener to that voice. Think about that for a second. If there's a voice talking in your head, and you can hear it, that means there are two beings involved. The speaker and the listener. You are the listener. You are the observer. The egoic voice is the speaker. Recognizing that separation, that you are not your thoughts but rather the one observing your thoughts, changes everything. Because once you realize that, you stop identifying with every thought that pops into your head. You stop believing that every doubt, every fear, every limiting belief is the truth. You start to see them for what they are: just thoughts. Just noise. Just the ego doing its job. And you, the observer, get to choose which thoughts to listen to and which ones to let pass by.

The "But What If I Did?" Rebuttal

Here's a mental exercise that's going to help you manage your ego when it steps in to shut you down. And this one's powerful because it uses your subconscious in your favor instead of against you.

Let's say I'm doing my affirmations and I say, "I am a millionaire" ten times. And immediately, my ego steps in and says, "No, you're not. You know what it would take to be a millionaire. You've never done that before. You're not a millionaire." And that voice has access to all the receipts from your subconscious data bank. It's got proof that I'm not a millionaire.

So here's what I do. Instead of combating these triggered egoic responses, instead of trying to override that negative feeling, knowing I'll never be able to convince it because it has all that proof, I ask a question: "But what if I did?" or "But what if I was?"

Try it right now. Say to yourself, "I am a millionaire." Notice what your ego says. Then ask, "But what if I was?"

And here's why that works. Did you notice that when you ask yourself a question, your subconscious will automatically try to answer it as honestly as it can? This can be both a good thing or a bad thing. Let's use it for some good. When I ask, "But what if I were a millionaire?" My subconscious starts searching for an answer.

And honestly? If I were a millionaire, it would feel amazing. I'd feel lighthearted. I'd feel free. I'd feel different about everything around me. I'd walk differently. I'd talk differently. I'd carry myself with a different energy. I heard a line in a song once where they said, "A couple million makes you stand differently." That is one hundred percent true. When you have that kind of abundance, it changes everything about how you move through the world.

And that's the feeling I want to sit in. That's the frequency I want to vibrate at. Because we are tuning forks. And when I vibrate at the frequency of being a millionaire, not worrying about money, feeling abundant, feeling free, that's when I start attracting that reality into my life. And that's the goal. How long can you sit in that frequency before the ego disrupts it in an attempt to bring you back to this moment? And then once it does do that, do you pull yourself back to that frequency using a rebuttal or not? That's your winning formula. That's your new daily practice for limiting beliefs.

And here's what happens next. Once you start feeling that abundance, that lightheartedness, that freedom, your brain starts to shift. Your brain will start throwing these great feelings at you throughout the day. Instead of constantly reminding you of what you don't have, it starts showing you glimpses of what it would feel like to have it. And the more you practice this rebuttal, the more those positive feelings show up, your algorithm shifted to autopilot.

So the "But what if I did?" rebuttal isn't about convincing your ego that you're right. It's about shifting your focus from what you don't have to how it would feel to have it. And that feeling is what creates the vibration. And that vibration is what pulls the coin toward you.

Like I said, try it. If your ego whispers that you'll never be successful after you do a positive affirmation, you say, "But what if I was?" Stop for a second. Really feel the answer to that question. Don't just think it. Feel it. You might only get one to three seconds before the ego kicks in with more rebuttals. But that's when you implement your next rebuttal. "How would that feel?" And now you're back in that high vibration for another few seconds. You're maximizing the time you spend vibrating at the frequency you want to attract into your life.

Ego says, "You don't have what it takes." You say, "But what if I did?" Pause. Feel it. "What would life look like?"

Ego says, "People like you don't win." You say, "But what if I did?" Pause. Feel it. "What would it feel like to have won?" (today)

You're not arguing. You're redirecting. You're opening a door. And when you do that repeatedly, the ego starts to back off. And here's why. It's like programming. Your ego is used to you thinking a certain way thousands of times a day. That's the pattern it knows. That's the algorithm it runs. But when you start using this rebuttal consistently, you're interrupting that algorithm. You're creating a new neural pathway. And the more you reinforce it, the more authentic and stronger it becomes. Eventually, your brain defaults to the new pattern instead of the old one. That's not wishful thinking. That's neuroscience. That's how you reprogram your subconscious to work for you instead of against you.

Managing the Ego with Your Best Next Shot

Here's why the ego freaks out when you try to manifest something big, and how focusing on your best next shot helps you sidestep that resistance.

Let's say you're making $50,000 a year and you suddenly start affirming, "I'm a millionaire." Your ego immediately pulls up your bank statements, your tax returns, your job title, your current lifestyle, everything in your subconscious database that proves you're not a millionaire. And it throws all of that evidence at you. "See? You're lying. Stop it." The gap between where you are and where you're claiming to be is too big. Your ego can't accept it. And that creates a huge element of resistance.

But here's what happens when you focus on your best next shot, your next achievable milestone, instead of the final score. If this were basketball, it'd be intensely focused on nothing except your next shot. Not your total points that you will have at the end of the game, or whether you will win the game or not. Just that very next shot.

If you're making $50,000 and you start affirming, "I'm making $60,000 this year," your ego looks at that and says, "Okay, that's a small stretch, but it's not impossible. We've seen people get raises. We've seen promotions. This could happen." There's less resistance. Less pushback. And that creates space for your manifestation to take root and grow.

And once you hit $60,000? You're not making $50,000 anymore. You've upgraded your reality. Your subconscious database has updated. And now when you aim for $75,000, your ego says, "Well, we just went from $50k to $60k. Going to $75k isn't that crazy of an idea."

Each milestone you hit strengthens your belief in your Ability To Manifest. And that confidence makes the ego less reactive, almost like it stays asleep while you're working. It's not constantly butting in because what you're claiming is within the realm of believability based on your track record. You're not asking it to believe something ridiculous. You're asking it to believe in the next logical step, which is key.

It's like Will Smith talks about when he was building a brick wall with his father. His dad told him, "Don't worry about the wall. Just lay this brick as perfectly as a brick can be laid." That focus on the next brick, not the entire wall. The ego can handle stairs. It can't handle leaps because your ego has never seen you do that. You are not used to seeing someone leap from the bottom floor to the top floor of a building. And because you've never witnessed it, your ego treats it as impossible.

So focus on your best next shot. Not the ultimate destination. The next brick in the wall. Because every time you hit that next milestone, you strengthen your belief in your Ability to Manifest. And that proof makes the next milestone easier to believe in and then achieve.

Seeing Your Ego Differently

Here's another way to think about the ego, and this came to me while reading a book called The Untethered Soul by Michael Singer.

Imagine you're standing in a press conference room full of reporters. And every single one of them is raising their hand, shouting questions or suggestions at you. "What about this? What about that? You can't do that. What if you fail? What if you end up looking stupid?"

They're all yelling at the same time, trying to get your attention. That's your ego. It's like a room full of reporters, all of them demanding that you listen to them, answer their questions, and validate their concerns. But here's the thing. You don't have to listen to all of them. You don't have to answer every question. You don't have to give them your attention because they're loud and sometimes come with proof.

You can look at that room full of reporters and say, "I know what you're all about. I don't have time for that." Self-preservation aside, for my health and safety, I know what you're all about, and I don't have time for that.

And the voices don't stop. They're always going to be there. That's part of life. That's part of being human. The chatter in your head, the doubts, the fears, the limiting beliefs, the what-ifs, they don't just disappear because you've read a book or done some mental exercises. Acceptance is a big part of this work. You have to accept what the ego is and that it's always going to show up. But you don't have to let it control you or your emotions or your decisions or your outcomes.

That's what it's like to manage your ego. You acknowledge it. You don't hate it. But you don't let it control you, either. The ego can be very loud and persistent. It thinks it's helping you. But it's also the thing that will keep you stuck if you let it. So learn to recognize its voice. Learn to say, "Thanks, but no thanks." And keep moving forward.

The ego isn't the enemy. It's just trying to protect you. But protection and growth don't always go hand in hand. Sometimes, you've got to step outside the bodyguard's comfort zone. And that's when the magic happens.

CHAPTER SIX:
ACCEPTANCE IS KEY
(THE RULES OF THE GAME YOU'RE IN)

You can't play a game to win if you don't both know and accept the rules. You can complain about the rules all you want. You can say they're unfair. You can wish they were different. But until you accept them, you're not in a good position to win. You're running around not knowing where out of bounds is, not knowing what the goal of the game is, or how to get there. Yeah, you're in the game, just like you're in the game of Law of Attraction with every thought you have, but without knowing the rules, you're lost.

And that's what most people do with the Law of Attraction. They hear about it. They get excited. They try it for a few days. And because it doesn't transform their lives in that short time, they say, "Well, I guess it doesn't work for me." Then they shrug their shoulders and give up. But they never actually accepted the rules of how it works. They never fully committed to understanding what they were getting into. They set themselves up to fail from the beginning.

So let me give you the rules I've learned so far. The real rules. Not the sanitized, feel-good version you see in memes and Instagram posts. It's not just about being positive or just doing countless emotionless affirmations. This is the actual, sometimes uncomfortable truth about how this works. Once you learn and accept these rules, everything becomes not easy, but easier.

Controlling Your Thoughts

Let's start with the big one. Controlling your thoughts is the hardest occupation a man or woman can have, according to both science and religion. I've heard this from every great philosopher, spiritual teacher, and neuroscientist I've studied. They all agree on this one point: managing your thoughts is one of the most difficult things you will ever attempt to do.

Think about this. Picture your grandmother, grandfather, or relative in the hospital. You don't know what's wrong. You don't know if they're gonna make it out this time. The hospital bed's beeping, and you feel the wave of sadness, fear.

How hard would it be to stay positive and envision them making it home this time? And while you're trying to stay positive, the what-ifs just keep popping up.

And that's the reality of this work. You can know all the rules. You can understand how it works. You can be committed to working on controlling your thoughts. But life is still going to put you in situations where staying positive feels like the hardest thing in the world. You're working that muscle against everything your survival instincts are screaming at you.

Controlling one's thoughts is the hardest occupation a man could have. And in those moments, you've got to give yourself grace. You've got to accept that you're human. You've got to do the best you can.

But you also can't use that as an excuse to give up. You can't say, "Well, it's too hard, so I'm not even going to try." You try anyway. Even when it's hard. Especially when it's hard. Life is going to be life. Not everyone is going to live forever, and everything happens for a reason. We've all lost somebody. And acceptance of not only the rules of this game, but what happens in life is another level of acceptance that absolutely needs to be conquered in order to get anywhere with this whole Law of Attraction manifesting thing.

And here's why it's so hard. You have somewhere between 60,000 to 70,000 thoughts per day. And 94% or more of those thoughts are on autopilot. They're running programs, ideas, and thought processes that were installed years ago, some even decades ago. Programs you didn't consciously choose. Programs that were formed by your upbringing, your environment, your experiences, your traumas, your wins, your losses, all of it running in the background without you even realizing it.

So when someone tells you, "Just think positive," what they're really saying is to wake up from your autopiloted normal thought processes to this moment and choose more positive thoughts. Now, with around 65,000 thoughts on average per day per person, and 94% of them being on autopilot, trying to have a positive day, which could be the equivalent of 51% positive thoughts or greater, is no small task. That means consciously choosing better thoughts over 30,000 times. Every. Single. Day.

But here's the thing. To whom much is given, much is tested. This is the hardest occupation a man could have. But it yields the greatest reward, which is the ability to create your future. So yes, it's more than worth it.

Every second of each and every day of your lives these rules, much like gravity, are inescapably followed. He always says, "Show me your predominant thoughts and I'll show you your tomorrow." But controlling one's thoughts is the hardest occupation a man can have according to both science and religion. So yea, it'll be tough, then it'll get annoying, but well worth it if you make it your mission.

- From "The Resume"

You Do and Will Have Negative Thoughts (And That's Normal)

Here's where people get tripped up. They think that if they're doing this right, they won't have negative thoughts anymore. They think after the first week they're going to become problem-less, without life's complications, walking around smiling 24/7, never stressed, never worried, never afraid.

That's not real. That's not human. And anyone who tells you they've achieved that is either lying or they've been living in a monastery with no responsibilities, no job, no family, and no bills. And even then, they still have to worry about their personal health and whatever crops they're going to harvest for food.

You are going to have negative thoughts. Every single day. Multiple times a day. And that's okay. That's normal.

Here's one of my biggest pet peeves. So many people tell me they're not negative. Then they tell me they don't have negative thoughts. And that's just a lie. Because as humans, self-preservation is one of the foundational components of every thought that we have. We are constantly scanning our environment for threats. We are always thinking, "What could go wrong? What do I need to protect myself from? What danger am I not seeing?"

That's not a flaw. That's a survival instinct. That's self-preservation. And that creates negative thoughts. So stop expecting that after the first week or month, you'll never have a negative thought again. Stop beating yourself up when you catch yourself worrying, stressing, or doubting. That's exactly what you were meant to be thinking about in that current moment. You know how I know? Because that's what happened. So don't beat yourself up if you lack doing your mental exercises today or if you find yourself stressing a lot.

That's part of the game. The goal isn't to eliminate negative thoughts. The goal is not to let them run the show. The goal is to catch them by acknowledging them and then redirect.

Own Your Stuff

Which brings me to the hardest rule to accept. Everyone's manifesting. All day, every day, we're all manifesting, good and bad, every year, all of our lives. You have to own your stuff. You have to take responsibility for everything in your life. Not just the good stuff. Everything.

When something bad happens, when you get a nasty email, when someone disrespects you, when you lose money, when things don't go your way, your first instinct should be to ask yourself, "What did I do to manifest this?" Not in a self-blaming, shameful, guilt-ridden way. But in an honest, curious, "let's not do that again" preemptive way.

Because here's the truth. If you manifested the good stuff in your life, your job, your home, your relationships, then you also manifested the bad stuff. You can't pick and choose. You can't say, "I manifested the promotion, but I didn't manifest the toxic coworker." Yes, you did. Maybe not consciously. Definitely not on purpose. But somewhere in your thoughts (emotions), in your energy, in your frequency, you expected/allowed that into your life. Something about your previous experiences on this earth has led you to believe that this part of your life is going to be consistent, at least for this next turn.

And I know that's hard to hear. I know it feels unfair. But once you accept it, it's actually empowering. Because if you created it with your thoughts (emotions), you can change it with your thoughts (emotions). But you've got to own it first. You've got to stop shooting the messenger. When life shows you something you don't like, don't get mad at life. Don't get mad at the universe. Don't get mad at the person or situation that's reflecting your energy back at you. Look in the mirror and ask, "What have I been thinking about or focusing on, or expecting that either has created or is creating this situation?"

Own Your Stuff Audit

Here's your mental exercise for this chapter. When something goes wrong in your life, I want you to pause and ask yourself one question in an honest, curious way: "What have I been thinking about in the last few days and weeks to manifest this situation?"

And then adjust accordingly. Don't sit there and worry about it. Figure out what to do to make sure this changes for the future. Because the more you worry about it, the more stuff like that's going to continue to happen to you, equaling the energy that you're putting out into the world/universe. Third law of motion, baby!, it will come back to you.

Maybe you've been stressing about money, and then an unexpected bill shows up. You manifested that. Maybe you've been complaining about your job, and then you get written up. You manifested that. Maybe you've been doubting your relationship, and then your partner picks a fight. You manifested that too. I know some people are gonna say my bills are coming, regardless. But you being in a situation of stress about your bills is something you're manifesting, in addition to your expectation that your bills are coming. Yes, it's safe to expect that your bills are on their way, but you don't have to expect it to be a struggle to pay them all the time.

I'm not saying you wanted those things. I'm saying you were focused on them. And whether you focus on having debt or not having debt, your focus is on debt. And debt will grow in your life. You were focusing on them enough. You watered that seed enough to manifest this into your life again. So own it. Acknowledge it. And then make a conscious decision to shift your focus to something better.

Because you can't change what you don't take responsibility for. And if you keep blaming everyone and everything else for your problems, you're giving away your power. You're saying, "I'm a victim. I have no control. Life just happens to me." And if that's the energy you're putting out, that's the reality you're going to keep experiencing.

But if you own your stuff, if you say, "I created this, and I can create something different," then you take your power back. And that's when everything changes.

Don't Ask, Demand

Here's something that changed everything for me once I understood it. You don't ask the universe for anything. Ever. You demand it.

And I don't mean demand in a harsh, angry, entitled way. I mean demand the way you command your hand to pick up a fork at dinner. You don't sit there and say, "Hand, would you please pick up this fork? I'd really appreciate it if you could help me out here." You don't ask permission.

You don't beg. You don't hope your hand cooperates. You just command it. Simple. Natural. No hesitation.

That's the energy you need when you're manifesting. You're not asking the universe if maybe, possibly, if it's not too much trouble, you could have what you want. You're claiming it. You're demanding it. Because it's already yours.

Think about it like this. Imagine you're carrying a heavy, fragile box. Your dog comes running up to you, trying to play, blocking your path. You don't stop and say, "Hey buddy, would you mind moving? I'd really appreciate it." You just say, "Move." Firm. Clear. Direct. And the dog moves. You're not being harsh. You're not being disrespectful. But you are making a command that you expect to be followed.

That's the energy of manifestation. It's not wishful thinking. It's not hoping. It's not asking. It's claiming what's already yours with the confidence and certainty that it will show up.

When you ask, you're operating from a place of lack. You're saying, "I don't have this, and I need you to give it to me." When you demand, you're operating from a place of ownership. You're saying, "This is mine. I'm calling it in now."

That shift in energy changes everything. Because the universe doesn't respond to begging. It responds to certainty. It responds to ownership. It responds to the person who moves through life as if they already have what they want, because energetically, they do.

So stop asking. Start demanding. Claim what's yours. And watch how fast the universe delivers.

This is hard. I'm not even gonna lie to you and say that it's in the slightest way easy, but it's worth it. But accepting that it's hard is just another level of acceptance you're going to have to adapt to if you want to fully be able to use all this to your advantage. You could even actually start to expect it to be easy if you can alter your brain algorithm in that way, and it will become easier. But that's only a master class level.

Because you stop fighting reality. You stop resisting. You stop wishing it were different. And you start working with what is.

That's when you stop being a victim of your thoughts and become the architect of them. That's when the real transformation begins.

CHAPTER SEVEN:

YOUR ATM

(THE ONLY SKILL THAT ACTUALLY MATTERS)

Let me tell you about the day that changed everything for me. March 11, 2008. That's the day I first watched *The Secret*.

I was a cop in Camden, New Jersey. At the time, it was ranked the poorest and most dangerous city in America. I'm talking about a place where I got hurt every single year I was on the force. Broken bones, injuries, fights every night. I was chasing people in cars and on foot, most days hourly. It was a war zone. Corruption in the police department that would rival movies you may see about New York or Chicago. This is a town whose chief of police is often fired and mayors are often removed due to corruption. Not just something made up. Runs deep and it's been running deep for years.

But I was obsessed with the brain. Always have been. Since I was a kid, I wanted to understand how people think, why they do what they do, how the mind works.

Times were tough. I was a single father raising two kids on my own. I was dealing with racist supervisors who were legitimately setting me up. I went above their heads to complain, and they would punish me further by doing things like transferring me from night shift to day shift, which totally screwed me up for home care for the children. I was surrounded by negativity, walking into the poorest houses I'd ever seen on a daily basis. My sister, who was a dispatcher in my police department, passed away. I had no relationship, no female in my life, and I was raising two kids on my own.

But I knew I was meant for more.

That's when my partner at the time told me he was a retired CIA agent. I never looked into it, but he was one of the smartest guys I'd met, so I believed him. One day he tells me there's a book they make all the CIA recruits read at the academy. He said, "You'd really enjoy it. It's called The Secret."

Now, I'm a SWAT-type guy. Rapid deployment. Man's man. Cop's cop. So when I went to pick up this movie called The Secret, I'm thinking it's going to be some tactical, SWAT-type thing.

It wasn't.

It was about the Law of Attraction. About how your thoughts shape your reality. About how what you focus on is what you create.

And I'm sitting there watching this movie, and puzzle pieces that have been missing my whole life just started clicking into place. It all made sense finally.

I Was Already Doing It (And Didn't Even Know It)

Here's what blew my mind: I realized I'd been using the Law of Attraction my entire life without knowing it.

In high school, I was a wide receiver on the football team. We didn't have Friday night games because of the fights and everything. We had Saturday morning games at like 10 a.m. I had to be in the locker room by like 7:30 a.m.

And every week I'd go out to the field early when nobody else was there. No crowd, no noise. Just me and the empty field. And I'd stand there near the goal post and visualize. I didn't know why I was compelled to do this before every game but I didn't question it either.

I'd see myself running a route. Ten yards, then out. Catch it. Boom. Quick slant. Catch it. Boom. Post pattern. Catch it. Boom. I'd visualize my offense marching down the field, making play after play, all the way to the end zone. Then I'd start over.

I'd do this over and over. And every now and then, one of my teammates would come outside and say, "Yo Neomaya, you good? (They all knew me by my whole name) What are you doing out here?"

And I'd say, "Just going over the playbook."

To them, I was just standing there staring at the grass. But in my mind, I was running plays. I was feeling the ball in my hands. I was there.

I never knew why I did that. I just felt like I had to.

When I saw The Secret, I realized what I'd been doing all along. I was visualizing. I was proactively manifesting. I was training my brain to expect success.

And it worked.

Eight Months

Given everything I was dealing with, the injuries, the corruption, being a single dad, I needed a way out. One day after getting injured on duty in a high rise building fight that turned into a fire evacuation, a short while later they just stopped paying me. Out of nowhere.

I started doing mental exercises every single day. Multiple times a day. I visualized being retired. I visualized having a pension. I visualized never having to work again. I said affirmations. I did the watcher exercise. I compounded everything I was learning. In the movie The Secret, the guy wrote a check to himself and did mental exercises with it every day. I did the same, came up with my own mental exercises that resonated with me. And it worked. There's a lot more involved, and I made it sound easy just now, but it worked.

And I did it with absolute certainty that it was going to happen.

I didn't wait for permission. I didn't wait for things to get easier. I didn't wait for a miracle. I manifested it.

By November 28, 2008, I worked my last day as a cop. I was retired. Permanently. With a pension. At 28 years old.

Eight months.

And the reason I was able to do that, the reason I went from a cop getting hurt every year to retired for life in eight months, is because I stopped focusing on the thing I wanted and started focusing on something way more powerful. I focused on my ATM. My Ability To Manifest.

What Is Your ATM?

ATM stands for Ability To Manifest. And it's the only skill that actually matters. Because once you build confidence in your Ability To Manifest, you can manifest anything. Any job. Any relationship. Any amount of money. Any experience. Anything.

Most people approach manifestation backwards. They focus on the specific thing they want. "I want a million dollars. I want a new car. I want a promotion. I want a spouse." And then they try to visualize that thing, affirm that thing, believe in that thing. And when it doesn't show up fast enough, they get discouraged. They think it's not working. They think maybe the Law of Attraction doesn't work for them.

But here's the problem with that approach. When you focus on a specific thing you don't have, your ego steps in and says, "No, you don't. Look around. You don't have a million dollars. You don't have that car. You don't have that job." And every time the ego does that, it chips away at your confidence. It reinforces the lack. It keeps you stuck.

But when you focus on your Ability To Manifest, everything changes. Because your Ability To Manifest isn't something you're trying to get. It's something you already have. You've been using it your whole life. You just didn't know it.

You've Already Manifested Things

Think about it. Your house, your apartment, your car. At one point in your life, they were all goals of yours. After achieved, eventually they will feel like stepping stones to your next goal. But at one point, they were all goals. You didn't always live there. You didn't always have access to it. But you thought about it; you worked toward it. And now it's your reality.

That's manifestation.

What are you wearing right now? At some point, you didn't own those clothes. You saw them, you wanted them, you acquired them. That's manifestation.

What's your job? At some point, you didn't have that job. You applied, you interviewed, you got hired. Those are all manifested steps in a manifestation process.

Who's in your life? Your partner, your kids, your friends. At some point, they weren't in your life. And now they are. That's manifestation.

You see where I'm going with this? You've already been manifesting. Your entire life is proof that you have the Ability To Manifest. The house you live in, the car you drive, the job you have, the people you know, all of it is evidence that your ATM works.

So instead of trying to manifest something you've never had before, which feels impossible to your ego, focus on the fact that you've already manifested things. And if you did it before, you can do it again.

My Manifestation Resume

Let me give you my manifestation resume. Because when I started to really look at my life, I realized I'd been manifesting big things for years without even knowing it.

I manifested getting hired as a cop in one of the most dangerous cities in America. That wasn't luck. That was me wanting it, focusing on it, and making it happen.

I manifested surviving some of the wildest, most dangerous situations you can imagine. High-speed chases. Foot pursuits. Physical altercations. Getting hurt every single year and still making it out alive. That wasn't luck. That was me expecting to be okay.

I manifested custody of my kids. I walked into a courtroom with no lawyer, spoke from my heart, and walked out with my kids under my roof every day of their lives until they became adults and moved out on their own. That wasn't luck. That was me knowing, deep down, that it was already mine.

I manifested winning the lottery thirteen times in the next year. Not millions. But thirteen wins. And every single time, I celebrated like I just hit the big jackpot. Because I was training my brain to see myself as a winner.

I manifested retirement at 28. With a pension. For life. Do you know how rare that is? Do you know how many people told me it was impossible? But I didn't listen to them. I focused on my Ability To Manifest. And I did.

And since then? I've manifested moving to Florida. I've manifested speaking on stages in front of thousands of people. I've manifested winning Dentistry's Got Talent, an international speaking competition, solidifying me as one of, if not the top speaker in dentistry. I've manifested connections with some of the most influential people in the industries I'm in. I've manifested this book. I've manifested a life that, ten years ago, I couldn't even imagine.

And none of that happened because I got lucky. It happened because I built confidence in my Ability To Manifest.

Why Focusing on Your Ability To Manifest Is a Game-Changer

When you focus on your Ability To Manifest instead of a specific goal, your ego has nothing to fight. Because you've already proven you can manifest things. You've already got a track record. You've already got evidence. So when you say, "I have the Ability To Manifest this," your ego can't argue. Because it's true.

And once your ego stops fighting you, once it stops throwing up resistance every time you try to think big, that's when the magic happens. That's when things start moving fast. That's when opportunities start showing up out of nowhere. That's when the universe says, "Okay, this person is serious. Let's give them what they're asking for."

ATM Confidence Builder

Here's your mental exercise for this chapter, and this one's going to be powerful. I want you to make a list. Write down ten things you've already manifested in your life. And I don't care how big or small they are. Just write them down.

Maybe it's your job. Maybe it's your home. Maybe it's your car. Maybe it's your relationship. Maybe it's your kids. Maybe it's a trip you took. Maybe it's an accomplishment you're proud of. Maybe it's surviving something you didn't think you'd survive. Anything. Just write down ten things that, at one point, didn't exist in your life, and now they do.

Because that's your proof. That's your evidence. That's your manifestation resume. And every time your ego tries to tell you that you can't manifest something, I want you to pull out that list and remind yourself: "I've done it before. I can do it again."

"I've Manifested Before, I Can Manifest Again"

Here's the second part of this exercise. I want you to say this affirmation ten times a day, every single day: "I've manifested before, and I can manifest again."

That's it. Simple. Powerful. And completely accurate. Your ego can't argue with it. Because it's true. You have manifested before. And you can manifest again.

And the more you say it, the more your brain starts to believe it. The more you believe it, the more you expect it. And the more you expect it, the more it shows up.

This isn't just about positive thinking. This is about building unshakable confidence in your Ability To Manifest. And once you have that confidence, nothing can stop you.

So when the chips were down, he was up! When life told him he was stuck, he screamed, "NO I'm in control of my thoughts."

"And since thoughts become things, I have all control. That makes sense, but that's not what I've been taught."

-From "The Resume"

Your Ability To Manifest is the only skill that actually matters. Because once you master it, you can create anything. And the best part? You've already been using it your whole life. Now it's time to use it on purpose.

CHAPTER EIGHT:
EXPECTATION CREATES YOUR REALITY

Let me tell you the real secret that nobody talks about. It's not affirmations. It's not visualization. It's not gratitude. Those things help, but they're not the thing that actually creates your reality.

It's expectation.

What you truly expect, deep down in your core, buried deep in your subconscious, which you cannot access, is what you're going to get. Not what you hope for. Not what you wish for. Not what you pray for. What you expect.

And here's the formula for how expectations get created:

The more you say something, the better ideas your brain comes up with to support it. The better ideas your brain comes up with, the more you start to believe it. The more you believe it, the more you expect it. And the more you expect it, the more it shows up in your reality.

Say it more → Better ideas → Belief → Expectation → Reality.

That's how your brain works. And once you understand this, everything else will make sense and you'll be able to use it to your advantage.

Confidence = Expectation

Let me break this down even further. Confidence isn't just feeling good about yourself. Confidence is expecting a specific outcome.

When you're confident you're going to get the job, you walk into that interview differently. You speak differently. You carry yourself differently. And because of that, you're more likely to get the job. Not because you were faking it. Because you genuinely expected it.

When you're confident you're going to win the game, you play differently. You take risks you wouldn't normally take. You make moves you wouldn't normally make. You may even put more on the line. Higher risks, higher rewards. And because of that, you're more likely to win.

When you're confident you're going to succeed in business, you show up differently. You invest differently. You network differently. And because of that, you're more likely to succeed.

Confidence isn't just a feeling. It's an expectation. And expectation is what creates reality.

So the question isn't "How do I feel more confident?" The question is "What do I actually expect to happen?" Because whatever you expect is what's going to show up.

And here's the key to building that expectation: you don't ask for what you expect. You demand it.

When you truly expect something, you're not sitting around hoping it shows up. You're not crossing your fingers and wishing for the best. You're claiming it. You're demanding it the same way you demand your legs to carry you when you stand up. You don't ask your legs, "Hey, would you mind holding my weight today?" You just stand. You expect them to work. You demand that they work without even thinking about it.

That's the energy of expectation. It's certain. It's firm. It's already done in your mind. And when you carry that energy, when you demand what you want instead of asking for it, you shift from hoping to knowing. And knowing is what creates reality.

Walking Around Broke Like Royalty

Let me tell you a story that illustrates this perfectly. There was a time in my life when I was dead broke. I'm talking about negative bank account balances. I'm talking about $127 to my name and rent due in three days. I'm talking about going to the grocery store with my kids and having to put things back at the register because I didn't have enough money.

But here's the thing. Even in those moments, I walked around like royalty. I'm not saying I was arrogant. I'm saying I carried myself like someone who expected good things to happen. I smiled at people. I talked to strangers. I acted as if I belonged everywhere I went.

And people responded to that energy. Opportunities showed up. Connections were made and doors opened. The universe had no choice but to respond to my energy output. Not because I had money, but because I expected to have money. And that expectation changed how I moved through the world, which then changed how the world moved around me.

There's a Drake lyric that captures this perfectly. He said his mother wonders where his mind is, his account's in the minus, but yet he rolls around the city like Your Highness. I want to partially credit the vibe of that song and those particular lyrics for keeping my head on straight and allowing me to hold my head that high while my account was literally in the negative. That was me. Broke as heck, but walking around with the energy of someone who knew, truly knew, that it was temporary. That it was just a chapter. That the next chapter was going to be completely different.

And it was.

The ShopRight Story

Here's another example. There was a grocery store I used to go to called ShopRight. And I remember one day in particular. I had my kids with me. We needed food. And I had maybe $30 to spend. That's it. For a week's worth of groceries for three people.

This was a time when I could have and should have been depressed, sad, scared for the future. I was caring for two children. My son was barely walking and my daughter just a few years older. And my kids were cranky. They were hungry. I was starving. And their mother was nowhere to be found.

With all that going on, all that happening, I could feel myself starting to spiral. Starting to think about how hard life was. How unfair it was.

How I didn't deserve to be in this situation. But then something sparked in me that chose to say, "I can't continue to think like this. I can't continue to be like this. I can't continue to move like this mentally." I stopped. I took a breath. And I made a decision. I was going to be happy in this moment. Not happy about the situation. But happy in spite of it.

So I started joking with my kids. Making them laugh. Playing games while we shopped. Acting like we were on some kind of adventure instead of a survival mission. And you know what? By the time we left that store, we were all in a better mood. We were all lighter. We were all expecting things to get better.

And they did.

But here's what I want you to understand. That shift didn't happen because I suddenly had more money. It happened because I shifted my expectation. I stopped expecting struggle and started expecting joy. And that change altered my course. Thoughts become things. Had I continued down that negative headspace, things would have gotten worse. And that is the only reason that pulled me out of the dumps.

These were the pivotal times in my life where I was waking up to the moment and saying to myself, "I can't sit in this headspace, or it's going to make things significantly worse." And repeatedly doing that is what conditioned me to start doing that more often in other situations. And when you expect joy, even in the middle of struggle, joy starts showing up more often.

99% of Small Businesses Fail (Because They Expect To)

Here's a statistic that drives me crazy. They used to say that 99% of small businesses fail within the first few years. Not because starting a business is impossible. Because 99% of people who start businesses expect to fail.

Every small business owner may portray confidence in what's going to happen with this new company to his family and friends. But deep down inside, we know the percentage of small businesses that fail, and opening day wasn't anywhere as good as he planned or hoped it would be. Despite what smile he shows on his face, expectations are the reason why these small businesses fail. And he's never gotten that before.

They've heard the statistic. They've internalized it. And now they're walking into their business with the expectation that it probably won't work out. That all consuming percentage and thought process wins and guess what? They end up being just another statistic. There are dozens of other manifesting factors involved, but the outcome is statistically the same.

But what about that 1% who did succeed? You think they're smarter? More talented? More connected? Maybe. But more than anything, they expect to succeed. They don't see failure as an option. They don't entertain the possibility that it might not work. They expect it to work. And because they expect it, they're vibrating at and pulling closer towards them that level of success.

Remember back in Chapter 3 when we talked about the coins on the table and tuning forks? When you think about something you want, you start vibrating at the same frequency as that thing. And any two things that vibrate at the same frequency naturally pull towards each other. That's not just a metaphor, that's how energy works. When you expect success, you're vibrating at the frequency of success. And success starts moving toward you. When you expect failure, you're vibrating at the frequency of failure. And that's what shows up.

That's the difference. It's not luck. It's not talent. It's expectation.

What Do You Truly Expect?

Here's the hard question you need to ask yourself. What do you truly expect to happen in your life?

Not what you hope for. Not what you want. Not what you say out loud to other people. What do you actually, deep down, expect?

Do you expect to be successful? Or do you expect to struggle?

Do you expect to be wealthy? Or tomorrow, do you expect to wake up to your current situation again?

Here's what I mean by that. If I ask someone, "Do you expect to be wealthy?" I know they're going to say, "Yeah, I expect to be wealthy." But do you expect to wake up to that tomorrow? Or do you expect to wake up in the same financial situation you're in today? Let's be real about it.

Maybe you're hoping or even expecting to be in a different situation a year from now. But expecting to be in a different situation a year from now only manifests expecting to be in a different situation a year from now every year. Which means you never get it.

Do you expect to be healthy? Or tomorrow, do you expect to wake up with the same aches and pains as you do today?

Do you expect to be successful easily and effortlessly? Or do you expect there to be a bunch of hurdles to your success because that's what your experience in life has been?

Do you expect to be loved? Or do you expect to be alone?

Be honest. Because what you expect is what you're going to get.

And here's the tricky part. Most people don't even realize what they expect. They say they expect good things. But if you look at their thoughts, their actions, their energy, and the way they move, they're expecting the opposite.

They say they expect to get the job, but they're already planning what they'll do when they don't get it. I'm a fan of back up plans, but mentally you shouldn't spend a majority of your time there.

They say they expect to find love, but based on previous experiences they're already convinced all the good ones are taken.

Think about it. Most people's goals are to end up in a successful relationship or married. If you've had seven spouses, and none of them worked out, confidence wise and expectation wise you're batting zero out of seven. Your subconscious is using that 0 for 7 statistic to shape your expectations on what's going to happen with your next relationship. Same goes for inventions, startup businesses, and all kinds of ventures.

In life, we have these goals: get married, have a successful business, lose weight. But they're "end all, be all" goals. Getting married is the epitome, the top notch of a relationship. And every person we met where it didn't work out, goes on the "subconscious scorecard" as a loss. It's just like every business venture you've tried since your first one. Every diet or attempt at losing weight or gym membership. If you don't have six pack abs right now, your brain kind of chalks it off as a loss. And if you've never had a six pack, your subconscious holds that as the standard.

Most people say that they expect to be successful, but they're already preparing for failure.

Your words don't matter. Your expectations do.

The Expect-7 Challenge

Here's your first mental exercise for this chapter. I want you to pick one thing you're trying to manifest right now. Just one. It could be money. A job. A relationship. Health. Anything.

And for the next seven days, I want you to say this statement out loud, every single day: "I expect [insert goal here]."

Not "I hope." Not "I want." Not "I wish." "I expect."

"I expect this promotion."

"I expect financial freedom."

"I expect to meet great people."

"I expect to be healthy and strong."

Say it ten times as an affirmation. Say it in the morning when you wake up. Say it in the afternoon when doubt creeps in. Say it at night before you go to bed.

And here's the key. Don't just say the words. Feel the expectation. Feel what it's like to expect something the same way you expect the sun to rise tomorrow. The same way you expect gravity to work when you drop something. The same way you expect your car to start when you turn the key.

That's the level of expectation I'm talking about. Unshakable. Undeniable. Certain.

Do this for seven days straight and watch what happens. Watch how your brain starts coming up with ideas to support that expectation. Watch how opportunities start showing up. Watch how your energy shifts. Because expectation is magnetic. And when you truly expect something, the universe has no choice but to deliver it.

Confidence Algorithm Check

Here's your second mental exercise. This one's going to require some brutal honesty. I want you to check in with yourself and ask this question: "What do I truly expect to happen?" Not what you want to happen. Not what you hope will happen. What do you actually expect?

If you're trying to manifest money, ask yourself: "Do I expect to be wealthy, or do I expect to be in the same financial situation tomorrow as I am today?" If you're trying to manifest a relationship, ask yourself: "Do I expect to find love, or do I expect to be disappointed?" If you're trying to manifest a business, ask yourself: "Do I expect this to succeed, or do I expect it to fail?"

And don't lie to yourself. Don't give me the answer you think you're supposed to give. Give me the real answer. The one you feel in your gut.

Because if your expectation doesn't match your goal, you're not going to get your goal. You're going to get your expectations.

And once you identify where your expectation is, you can start working on changing it. You can start using affirmations, visualizations, and mental exercises to shift your expectation to match what you actually want.

But you can't change what you're not aware of. So get honest. Check your expectations. And if it's not where it needs to be, start doing the work to shift it.

Expectations Trump Everything

Let me say this one more time because it's the most important thing in this chapter. Expectations trump everything.

You can do all the affirmations in the world. You can visualize every single day. You can journal, meditate, set intentions, say prayers, burn sage, carry crystals. But if you don't expect it to work, it won't work. It can't work. Cause what you truly expect will happen. Even with failure or loss.

No matter what you do or say, if deep down inside you truly expect it not to work, it won't.

Because expectation is the final filter. It's the last checkpoint before something manifests into your reality. And if your expectation says "no," nothing else matters.

Now, I want to be clear about something. Just because expectation is the final step doesn't mean things manifest instantly once you finally expect them. The expectation has to be maintained. That seed has to be watered for a period of time. You need to vibrate at that frequency for a period of time before that thing manifests into your reality. Once you expect it, you have to sit in that expectation for a little while. It'll come in God's or the universe's time.

Side note: I reference God sometimes, sometimes I reference universe, sometimes I say God/universe. I simply do that so as not to offend anyone and for reference, the being I'm mentioning for those who have different beliefs. For those who don't believe in God or don't want to call it universe, I just say whoever you believe is creating everything, has created everything, and is creating everything as we go. That's the being I'm referencing.

That's why building confidence in your Ability To Manifest is so important. Because when you have confidence in your ability to manifest, you expect things to work out. You expect opportunities to show up. You expect the universe to deliver.

And when you expect it, it happens. Every single time.

Every second of each and every day of your lives these rules, much like gravity, are inescapably followed. He always says, "Show me your predominant thoughts and I'll show you your tomorrow."

— **From "The Resume"**

What you expect is what you get. So the question is: what are you expecting? And is that expectation creating the life you want, or the life you're trying to escape?

CHAPTER NINE:

AFFIRMATIONS

(THE RIGHT WAY AND THE WRONG WAY)

Let me tell you why most affirmations don't work. You stand in front of a mirror, look yourself in the eyes, and say, "I am rich. I am successful. I am confident." And immediately, something shifts inside your chest. A feeling of unease. A feeling that says, "No, you're not."

That's your ego. And it's just doing its job. Because what you just said wasn't true. And when you say something that's not true, your ego throws evidence at you. "You're not rich. Look at how you feel when you're doing affirmations for big goals and big dreams."

And just like that, your affirmation backfired. Instead of building you up, it tore you down. Instead of creating confidence, it reinforced doubt. Instead of manifesting what you want, it manifested more of what you don't want.

Remember from Chapter 2, every thought sits on a foundation. And if your thought foundation is "I'm not worthy" or "I'm not capable," no amount of pretty affirmations will override that. You're trying to build a mansion on quicksand. And it doesn't matter how beautiful the mansion looks; if the foundation is weak, it's going to crumble.

So let me show you how to do affirmations the right way. The way that actually works. The way that bypasses your ego and reprograms your brain without triggering resistance.

The Knot in Your Chest Test

There's a knot in your chest. It's there at all times. We're normally numb to it because it's always there, but it's one of the most powerful tools you have for testing whether an affirmation will work or not.

Here's how it works: When you say something positive that's true, something that makes you happy, that knot races up toward your throat. In my mind, it gives off an aura color like a blue, fading to a pure white the higher up it gets. The happier I am in that moment, the higher it goes.

But when you tell yourself a lie? The knot drops down. It turns red in my mind. It feels like discomfort, maybe even pain.

So here's the test: Say an affirmation out loud and pay attention to what happens. Does the knot go up or down?

If you say something like "I'm a billionaire" and you feel the knot in your chest drop down or feel uneasy at the very least, you know your ego's not agreeing with it. Your ego is going to pull you out, throw receipts at you, do everything it can to bring you back to this current moment and away from whatever daydream reality it believes you to be in.

And here's what's really happening: When you tell yourself that lie and your ego steps up and says "that's a lie" and proves it to you with your bank statement, you're now watering the seed of "I lie to myself about my financial situation, and it's way worse than I let it on to be when I'm having conversations with myself, causing internal struggle." You're manifesting more of that into your life.

Often, you only have to change just one word in your affirmation to cause it to go up instead of down.

Alternatively, regardless if you're rich or poor, try saying this: "I love money."

It's an accurate statement. Therefore, the ego is going to sit quiet. The subconscious is going to co-sign on the fact that you love money because you do. It feeds your family. And that knot in your chest is going to raise up towards a better, happier, feel-good place. You spend more and more time in this headspace, vibrating at this frequency. And as a tuning fork, you're attracting towards you a lifestyle situation where you're walking around with the mindframe of "I love money."

You see how just a few words can dramatically alter the meaning behind what you're saying, the feeling behind what you're saying, what you're manifesting next, and the vibrational frequency you're vibrating at, all of that.

That's the difference. Accurate statements vs. lies. One works. The other doesn't.

The Meditation Breakthrough

Now I'm going to tell you my story about how I used this principle to completely transform my meditation practice.

When I first started meditating, I hated it. According to psychology, the average person can't sit quietly in a quiet room in a chair for more than a couple of seconds before getting antsy, getting up and walking out, or picking up their phone. Psychology calls it mental torture. It's the current state of mind of almost everyone on the planet today.

If you want to quiet the mind, you must first practice quieting the mind. So when I sat still to quiet my mind, random thoughts would pop into my head, like "I have to get milk on the way home" and things of that nature. And I would shoo away that thought, like a pet yearning for my attention while I'm in an important business meeting. I'd shoo that thought away. I'd get back grounded, get back home to be present in the absence of thought, and two or three seconds later another thought would come in.

And that's what made it torturous to me. Because I had never attempted this before, which I equate to shooting a BB gun at a freight train and attempting to slow it down.

For the first fourteen days, attempting to meditate was torture. I was fighting it repeatedly. This torturous cycle of wake up, mental reel trap, wake up, mental reel trap is what ends up discouraging people from meditating in the first place. Not being able to stop their mind because they haven't practiced stopping their mind. Thus, the freight train analogy.

Your brain throws at you little short clips of different subjects and you're just entertaining them (like a reel trap), as opposed to realizing, "Wait a minute, I'm supposed to be meditating right now. Let me get back to that." And at first, you're not even good at that. You're not even good at recognizing that you're in another mental reel trap. Unless you're really good, you have just a few seconds before your brain throws at you another seemingly random thought. And that's what made it torturous.

But I wanted to be good at it. I wanted to experience what all these spiritual teachers were talking about. I wanted that peace, that clarity, that connection. Around day fourteen or fifteen, something told me to watch The Secret again. This time I keyed in on them saying "I'm so happy and thankful that I..." So I said to myself I'm going to try this for meditating.

I started saying, "I'm so happy and thankful that I'm good at meditating. I'm so happy and thankful that I enjoy meditating."

I kept doing those affirmations. And on day sixteen, it clicked. From day sixteen till today, meditating has been my favorite thing to do. Everybody knows, at least between midnight and two in the morning, almost every single night, I am meditating. And I look forward to it. I can't wait till my family goes to sleep and the phone calls and emails stop so that I can just engulf myself in self-discovery, peace, and stillness, and conversations with God, myself, ancestors, the walls, whoever or whatever I choose to point my thoughts/words and emotions at.

And I want to be clear, I don't want to mislead anyone into thinking I'm just sitting there in complete silence for four hours straight. There are several different types of meditation. The main one being complete absence of thought, which only lasts a few seconds before you have to keep resetting yourself. And then there's guided meditation where someone's maybe walking you through a peaceful forest. There are several different types. I do a bunch of them during those hours. There's also a level of proactive manifesting that I do in there too, which is like another form of meditating.

That transformation only happened because I reprogrammed my brain with an accurate affirmation that I repeated until it became true.

Lofty Questions (The Sneaky Way to Bypass Your Ego)

Here's another trick that works incredibly well. Instead of making a statement, ask a question. Your subconscious is programmed to answer questions. It can't help itself.

Let me give you an example. Let's say you want to eat healthier, but right now you're eating fast food four times a week. If you say, "I eat healthy all the time," your ego is going to shut that down immediately. Because it's not true.

But if you say, "Why do I eat so healthy?" your brain doesn't argue. When you ask yourself a question, the ego shuts up, enabling the subconscious to access its databank and look for the honest answer or reason. It starts coming up with answers. "Well, I ate a salad last Tuesday. I drink water sometimes. I had fruit for breakfast once this week." And the more your brain comes up with answers, the more it starts to believe the question is valid. And the more it believes the question is valid, the more it starts creating behaviors that match the question. And in trying to answer it, it starts reprogramming your behavior.

That's a lofty question. It's sneaky. It bypasses the ego. And it works.

Here are some examples:

"Why do I eat so healthy?" "Why am I so good with money?" "Why do people love working with me?" "Why am I so confident?" "Why does everything work out for me?"

Poison Words (And How to Reclaim Them)

You remember I mentioned that knot in your chest earlier? Well, there are certain words that almost always create that feeling of the knot dropping down. Words that I called "poison words" for years. Words like "can," "hope," and "will."

Here's why they're problematic:

When you say "I hope to get the promotion," you're manifesting a future (maybe one or two years from now or more) where you're still

91

saying "I hope I get the promotion," which means you never got it. You're programming yourself to stay in hope, not achievement.

When you say "I can do this," you're manifesting a future where you're still using "I can do this." Which means you haven't done it yet. You're stuck in possibility, not reality. "I will do this" works the same way. It keeps the thing perpetually in the future. It never arrives.

For fifteen years, I labeled these as poison words and tried to use them as seldom as possible. I trained myself to avoid them. And it helped.

But then something happened that changed my perspective. Someone asked me if I could run a multimillion dollar corporation. And without hesitating, I said, "Hell yeah, I can run a multimillion dollar corporation." And I felt the power in that statement. It wasn't weak. It wasn't uncertain. It was absolute conviction.

And I realized something important: If I didn't believe that statement, then it wouldn't have been powerful when I said it. But because I do believe that statement, because it's true to me in my core, it was so powerful and such a powerful use of the word "can" that I re-implemented that word back into my vocabulary.

So here's what I learned: These words aren't poison if you say them with absolute conviction. If you truly believe them. If there's no doubt behind them.

"I can" isn't poison if you genuinely know you're capable and making a demanding type statement being released into the universe.

"I will" isn't poison if you're stating an inevitable fact, not wishful thinking.

"I hope" might still be the weakest of the three, but even hope has its place when it's rooted in faith, not doubt.

The key is the energy behind the words. Not the words themselves.

So use these words carefully. Check your belief level. If there's any doubt, rephrase. But if you can say them with the kind of conviction I had when I said "Hell yeah, I can run a multimillion dollar corporation," then use them. Because at that point, they're not poison. They're fuel.

And that conviction? That's the energy of demanding. When I said, "Hell yeah, I can run a multimillion dollar corporation," I wasn't asking the universe for permission. I wasn't hoping it would agree with me. I was stating a fact. I was demanding that reality align with what I already knew to be true.

That's the difference between poison words and power words. It's not the word itself. It's whether you're asking or demanding. "I can" becomes poison when you're asking yourself if you're capable, hoping you are, wishing you were. But "I can" becomes fuel when you're demanding it as truth, declaring it with the same certainty you'd use to say your name.

Affirmations That Actually Work

Let me give you a list of affirmations that work because they're accurate. You can say these right now, in this moment, and your ego won't fight you.

"I deserve [insert goal here]." This is accurate. You do deserve good things. You deserve success, love, health and wealth. Your ego can't argue with that. You're not saying you have it. You're saying you deserve it. And you do.

"I love money." Accurate. You don't have to be rich to love money. Loving money is a choice. And when you say it enough, your relationship with money changes.

"How would it feel to [insert goal here]?" This is a question, so your ego doesn't fight it. And it gets you into the emotional state of already having what you want, which is the key to manifestation.

"Wouldn't it be awesome/amazing to [insert goal here]?" It's a question. It opens possibilities without making a false claim. Your brain starts imagining the scenario, and imagination is the first step to creation.

"I'm so happy and thankful that [insert goal here]." This one worked for me with meditation. It works because it's phrased as gratitude, and gratitude is a high-frequency emotion. Even if the thing isn't true yet, expressing gratitude for it shifts your energy.

"Yes." Just say "yes" ten times in a row. By the third time you say it, you should be smiling. By the fifth or sixth time, your brain starts coming up with reasons to say yes. It starts aligning with positivity, possibility, opportunity. It's simple. It's generic. And it works.

"Thank you." Say "thank you" ten times in a row. Your brain starts looking for things to be thankful for. And the more you're thankful, the more things show up in your life that you're thankful for.

These affirmations work because they're either accurate, phrased as questions, or expressed as gratitude. None of them trigger your ego to pull that knot in your chest down. And that's why they're effective.

Change Your Affirmations Often

Here's something most people don't realize. You're not supposed to use the same affirmation for the rest of your life. Affirmations are tools. And just like any tool, you use them for a specific job, and then you move on to the next one.

If you're trying to build confidence in your Ability To Manifest, you might use "I've manifested before, and I can manifest again" for a few weeks or months. But once that confidence is built, you don't need that affirmation anymore. You move on to something else.

If you're trying to improve your relationship with money, you might use "I love money" for a while. But once that relationship is solid, meaning you can speak on the subject with minimal egoic negative self-talk responses or limiting beliefs, you switch to something like, "Money flows to me effortlessly."

The key is to pay attention to what you need in the moment. What's the gap? What's the block? What's the belief that's holding you back? And then create an affirmation that addresses that specific issue.

Don't just pick one affirmation and repeat it for ten years. That's not how this works. Your life is constantly evolving. Your goals are constantly changing. Your affirmations should evolve with you.

The "Richard" Workaround

Let me give you an example of how I got creative with affirmations when I was trying to manifest wealth. I knew saying "I'm rich" wasn't going to work. The knot in my chest would drop immediately. So I came up with a workaround.

I started telling myself that my name was "Richard" and that "Rich" was my nickname. I told myself both to trick my ego into being quiet long enough for me to sit in that headspace, believing that Rich is the shorter version of Richard and overlooking the fact that neither was actually my name.

So I'd say, "I'm Rich."

Instead of my ego correcting me and saying "that's not your name," I found a way (mentally) to get it to focus on "Rich" being a shorter version of Richard. So it allowed me to sit in that headspace and associate my essence, my being, with the thought process behind what I grew up to think the word "rich" meant.

That's the kind of creativity you need when you're doing this work. If traditional affirmations don't work, find workarounds. Find a way to say something that bypasses your ego's resistance but still plants the seed you want to plant or causes you to vibrate at the frequency that best serves you and your purposes.

Mental Exercises for This Chapter

Here are the affirmations I want you to start using today. Pick two or three that resonate with you. Say them ten times each, every single day. And pay attention to how you feel when you say them. Pay attention to that knot in your chest. Does it go up or down? If it drops, adjust the wording until it rises.

"I deserve [insert goal here]." "I love money." "How would it feel to [insert goal here]?" "Wouldn't it be awesome/amazing to [insert goal here]?" "I'm so happy and thankful that/for [insert goal here]." "Why do I [positive trait]?" (Lofty question) "Yes." (Say it ten times, see what happens) "Thank you." (Say it ten times, feel the shift)

These are tools to reprogram your brain. The more you use them, the more your brain starts to believe them. And the more your brain believes them, the more your life starts to reflect them.

Affirmations work. But only if you do them right. Stop lying to yourself. Start using accurate statements. And watch how fast your life starts to change.

CHAPTER TEN:
COMPOUND EXERCISES
(AND WHY STACKING THEM CHANGES
EVERYTHING)

Most people think manifestation is one thing. You visualize. Or you affirm. Or you meditate. Or you express gratitude. And they do one of those things and wonder why nothing's happening.

But manifestation isn't one thing. It's everything at once. It's like baking a cake. You don't just throw flour in the oven and expect a cake. You need flour, sugar, eggs, butter, baking powder, milk. You need all the ingredients. And you need them in the right proportions, mixed together, at the right temperature.

That's what compound exercises are. You're not just visualizing. You're visualizing while feeling the emotions while adding physical sensations while bringing in the spiritual element. You're stacking layers. And when you stack enough layers, you don't create a small manifestation. You create a manifestation tidal wave.

Let me break down what I mean.

The Watcher Exercise

Let me tell you about the Watcher Exercise. It's one of the most powerful tools I've ever discovered, and it's one of my biggest contributions to why I was able to retire just eight months after learning about the Law of Attraction. Yes, the Law of Attraction is great, but some people call it the icing on top of the cake. I call it the icing on top of a multi-layered cake with sprinkles and jimmies and chocolate and all the fixings. This book is all of the ingredients in one place.

I was taking a government test once in a small room. There were no windows, no camera. It wasn't that important a test. Just four walls, a door, and a desk. No one else was in the room. It was the size of a large closet. I was done with the test. When I stood up to walk out of the room to let the people know I was done, I tripped, stumbled really, on the leg of the table. And I looked around with a feeling of embarrassment to see who saw me. Which was weird because I knew, and I took note when I first entered the room, that there were no cameras, no windows. No one could possibly have seen me. It wasn't an important enough situation for them to be recording.

So why did I look around? Why did I feel embarrassed? Who was I checking for?

That's when it hit me. There was something watching me. Not a person, not a camera, but something. An essence, a presence. And I could feel it. We've all felt it. At least once in our lives. They even wrote a song about it, Rockwell's "Somebody's Watching Me." It always feels like somebody's watching me.

Now, there are some people, in my experience particularly people from the hood, who say they don't know this feeling and they've never experienced it. And here's how I show them that they do know this feeling and they have experienced it. I'll ask them a question. And when they start to answer it, I say, "Pause. Don't move. Don't turn around. Stay right there." I go behind them, where they can't see me, and I set my phone on the counter or the bookshelf. Then I walk back to where I'm in front of them and they can see me again. I say, "Okay, go ahead. Finish telling me what you were telling me." And as soon as they start talking, I say, "Hold on. Just so you know, don't turn around, but I just put my phone on the counter and I'm live streaming to all of my Facebook fans right now. Don't turn around. Just go ahead and continue the story."

And when I tell people this, you can see it on their faces. They fight the urge to physically look over their shoulder at my phone and their audience. Because I told them not to turn around, they don't turn around, but you can see them go for it and then stop themselves. And then when they go to tell the story, they do what I call "tighten up." They start to correct everything. Their posture, what they're saying, their tone, to make sure that anyone who sees this video won't be able to hold anything against them in any way, shape, or form. And immediately, they feel the essence of their audience staring at them almost as a physical presence. They can feel what seems like a mental spotlight coming out of the front of the camera, beaming on them.

This is what I do for people who say they've never experienced this feeling before. Because there will be people reading this book who say they've never felt this feeling before. And I want you to know, we've all felt it. And that is the feeling that I woke up to in that moment. The feeling that I call the Watcher.

I like to study things that all people have in common. And when I first noticed the Watcher, I said to myself, "I've felt this essence watching me before. I know we all have this in common." So I decided to study this Watcher. And I made a discovery about this Watcher essence that I had just recently given a title to, after realizing that it was even there. The Watcher is watching at all times, even when you're not watching or paying attention to it.

That moment stuck with me. And I started paying attention to that feeling. I started noticing it more often. Started sitting in it, spending time with it, acknowledging it. And the more I did, the more powerful my manifestations became.

One of the things I noticed immediately about the Watcher was this: It knew that I had just said that. Which sparked something in me. Every time I pay attention or notice it watching me, it's already doing it. It's already watching me. And it knew that I had just made a decision to study it. Which means it can also hear my thoughts.

And I immediately thought to myself, "Hold on. Watching me at all times. Can hear my thoughts. Knows my intentions. That kind of sounds like God." And if I'm right, this is the closest us humans will come, or have come so far, to actually feeling God's essence on demand. To feel and interact with God. And I felt like I had made a breakthrough. Not of the century. But of mankind.

That really made me want to study it. So I did. I studied it more and more and more. And the biggest thing I learned about the Watcher was this: The more time I spent seeing, watching the Watcher watch me, the more powerful my manifestations were. The faster they came to me. The better the outcome.

What Compound Exercises Actually Are

When I say compound exercises, I'm talking about compounding exercises. Stacking them. Here's an example: Visualization, seeing yourself on the beach. Physical layer, your toes are physically in the sand in your backyard. That makes you feel like you're actually at the beach. That's the second layer. Emotional layer, enjoying it. That's adding an emotional layer, so it's not a hollow thought. Spiritual layer, adding in the Watcher, watching you enjoy yourself at the beach with your toes in the sand. That produces beach time.

When you spend time with the Watcher, you're spending time with God. You're aligning yourself with the creative force of the universe. You're signaling that anything's possible.

The Highest Version of Yourself

I read something in a book once that stuck with me. When you are smiling, when you are laughing, that's when you are most aligned with your higher self. Think of it like a hose with water going through it. You can either squeeze it, contract it, thus letting less water flow. Or you can expand it, letting more water flow. That flow, we're going to use that analogy for energy.

For all intents and purposes, let's say there are different versions of you. There's a highest version of you, higher versions of you, and lower versions of you that can exist. The highest version of you would be the equivalent of God, being one energetically. The lowest version of you would be the opposite. Laughing and feeling on top of the world, that's when you're vibrating at the same frequency, in alignment with and having the same thought processes as the highest version of you. And the same goes for the opposite.

And if you want your future to align with the highest version of yourself's future scenario, then you have to be vibrating at that frequency. Which means you have to be laughing or smiling. Obviously, we can't do that all day, every day. But the plan is to attempt to do it more often than not for better results. The more you are in that state, the more aligned you are with the creative force of the universe.

The Compound Exercise Template

Here's the template I use for every major manifestation:

Mental: What are you thinking? What are you visualizing? What scenario are you seeing in your mind? This is where most people stop. But it's just the first layer.

Emotional: How do you feel in this scenario? Not how you feel right now. How do you feel in the scenario you're visualizing? Are you happy? Excited? Grateful? Peaceful? Confident? You have to feel the emotion of the spirit experiencing it in this moment. If you can't feel it, your manifestation is hollow.

Physical: What are you doing with your body? Are you sitting? Standing? Walking? Moving? If you're manifesting success, maybe you're wearing nice clothes when manifesting that type of success. Maybe you're holding something that represents what you want. Maybe your toes are in the sand while you visualize the beach. The physical element grounds the visualization in reality.

Spiritual: This is where the Watcher comes in. You're not just visualizing the thing. You're feeling the presence of the Watcher watching you experience the thing. You're acknowledging that something greater than you is observing this moment. And that acknowledgment is what connects you to the creative force of the universe.

When you combine all four of these elements, mental, emotional, physical, spiritual, you create a manifestation tidal wave.

Visualizing the Boring Parts Too

Here's something most people miss. They visualize the highlight reel. The big moment. The achievement. The celebration. But they skip the boring parts. And the boring parts are what make it real.

Let me explain. If you're visualizing a trip to the Bahamas, most people visualize themselves on the beach. Sun setting. Waves crashing. Perfect moment. But they don't often visualize the flight, checking into the hotel, the elevator ride to their room, unpacking their suitcase, or waking up the next morning and brushing their teeth in the hotel bathroom. And those boring moments are what trick your brain into thinking you've already been there.

When I talk about tricking your brain, here's what I mean: Your brain doesn't know the difference between something you vividly imagined and something you actually experienced. It thinks that what you're visualizing is real. So it's sending off that frequency for you to receive back later on. And the proof is simple: it only takes a couple of seconds of sexual thought to cause an erection. Your body doesn't know you're not actually in that situation, so it responds accordingly and vibrates at that frequency.

That's why visualizing the boring parts is so important. Because when you visualize the elevator ride, the taxi, the quiet moments, your brain files those away as memories. And when you finally do take that trip, your brain says, "Oh, I've been here before." And that familiarity removes resistance. It makes the manifestation feel inevitable instead of impossible. So don't just visualize the big moments. Visualize the small ones too. The mundane ones. The in-between moments. Because those are the moments that make your brain believe it's real.

Don't Ask, Demand

Here's one of the biggest lessons I learned, and it changed everything. You don't ask the universe for anything. Ever. You demand it.

And I don't mean demand in a harsh, angry, entitled way. I mean demand the way you command your hand to pick up a fork at dinner. You don't sit there and say, "Hand, would you please pick up this fork? I'd really appreciate it if you could help me out here." You don't ask permission. You don't beg. You don't hope your hand cooperates. You just command it. Simple. Natural. No hesitation.

That's the energy you need when you're manifesting. You're not asking the universe if maybe, possibly, if it's not too much trouble, you could have what you want. You're claiming it. You're demanding it. Because it's already yours.

Think about it like this. Imagine you're carrying a heavy, fragile box. Your dog comes running up to you, trying to play, blocking your path. You don't stop and say, "Hey buddy, would you mind moving? I'd really appreciate it." You just say, "Move." Firm. Clear. Direct. And the dog moves. You're not being harsh. You're not being disrespectful. But you are making a command that you expect to be followed.

That's the energy of manifestation. It's not wishful thinking. It's not hoping. It's not asking. It's claiming what's already yours with the confidence and certainty that it will show up.

When you ask, you're operating from a place of lack. You're saying, "I don't have this, and I need you to give it to me." When you demand, you're operating from a place of ownership. You're saying, "This is mine. I'm calling it in now."

That shift in energy changes everything. Because the universe doesn't respond to begging. It responds to certainty. It responds to ownership. It responds to the person who moves through life as if they already have what they want, because energetically, they do.

So stop asking. Start demanding. Claim what's yours. And watch how fast the universe delivers.

November 2, 2008

Let me tell you about the day I put all of this together. It was November 2, 2008. I had just finished reading a book called *The Command,* and the principles in that book gave me a major leg up on manifesting. The book was essentially a list of mental exercises that all pointed to one thing: demanding what you want from the universe instead of asking for it. And that day, I decided to put it all together. The demanding, the visualizing, the Watcher, everything I had been learning since March. I had been doing mental exercises every single day since March. I had been visualizing, affirming, meditating. I had been using the Watcher. And on November 2nd, I brought it all together.

I sat down. I closed my eyes. And I visualized myself retired. Not just the idea of being retired. Not just the end result. I visualized the boring parts. I visualized waking up on a Tuesday morning with nowhere to be. I visualized making breakfast in my kitchen, slowly, without rushing. I visualized sitting on my couch in the middle of the day, just because I could. I visualized the freedom. The peace. The absence of stress. And while I was visualizing, I brought in the Watcher. I felt the presence of the Watcher watching me enjoy my retirement. Watching me live in peace. Watching me experience freedom. And I sat in that visualization for as long as I could. Feeling it. Living it. Experiencing it in my mind as if it were already real. And I demanded it. I claimed it as mine.

Twenty-six days later, on November 28th, was my last day working on the streets as a police officer. That's how powerful this is.

Compound Exercise Practices

Here's your mental exercise for this chapter, and it has two parts.

Part 1: The Watcher Practice

Ten times today, I want you to wake up from whatever task you're doing and just feel the Watcher watching you do that task. That's it. Just simply wake up from the moment. You can rub your thumb against your pointer finger and your middle finger, as if to symbolize how people would say "cash" back in the day. Use that to bring you back to this moment. And just feel the Watcher watching you. No good. No bad. Just feel the Watcher. Do this ten times today. And pay attention to what happens. Pay attention to how it feels. Pay attention to how your awareness shifts when you acknowledge the presence that's always been there.

Part 2: Compound Visualization

Pick one goal. Just one. And I want you to spend ten minutes visualizing it using all four layers:

Mental: What does the scenario look like? See it in detail. See it as happening right now.

Emotional: How does it feel? Don't just think about how it feels. Feel it. Right now. In this moment.

Physical: What are you doing with your body in this scenario? Stand up if you need to. Sit down, if you need to. Move if you need to. Make it physical.

Spiritual: Bring in the Watcher. Feel the presence of the Watcher watching you experience this moment. Acknowledge that something greater than you is observing this.

And here's the final step: Demand it. Don't ask for it. Don't hope for it. Demand it. Claim it as yours. Declare it with the same certainty you'd use to command your hand to move.

Do this for ten minutes. And when you're done, notice how different it feels compared to just visualizing alone. That's the power of compound exercises. You're not just thinking about what you want. You're living it. You're experiencing it. You're aligning with it on every level. And you're demanding it with absolute certainty. And when you do that, the universe has no choice but to deliver it.

CHAPTER ELEVEN:
PROACTIVE MANIFESTING
(LIVING IN YOUR FUTURE NOW)

Most people visualize once a day. Maybe in the morning. Maybe at night. They close their eyes, picture what they want for five or ten minutes, and then they go back to living in their current reality for the other 23 hours and 50 minutes of the day.

And they wonder why it's not working.

Here's the truth: If you spend five minutes a day visualizing your dream life and 23 hours and 55 minutes thinking about your current problems, your current limitations, your current reality, what do you think you're manifesting? You're manifesting more of what you're focused on 99.9% of the time. Which is your current reality.

That's where proactive manifesting comes in. Proactive manifesting isn't something you do once a day. It's something you live in. It's a state of being. It's spending as much time as possible mentally living in your future instead of your present.

And when you do that, when you truly commit to living in your future now, everything changes.

The Mental World vs. The Physical World

Let me explain how this works. There are two worlds you exist in simultaneously. The physical world and the mental world.

The physical world is where your body is right now. It's the room you're sitting in. The chair you're on. The phone or book in your hands. It's what's happening around you in this moment.

The mental world is where your mind goes when you close your eyes. It's where you dream. Where you imagine. Where you create scenarios that haven't happened yet. And here's what most people don't realize: The mental world is just as real as the physical world. Maybe more real. Because everything that exists in the physical world was created first in someone's mental world.

Your house, your car, your phone, the chair you're sitting on. All of it existed in someone's imagination before it existed in reality. Someone saw it in their mind first. Then they brought it into the physical world.

That's what you're doing with proactive manifesting. You're creating your future in your mental world first. And the more time you spend there, the faster it shows up in your physical world.

Neoland (Or Future Land, Or Whatever Feels Best)

I have a name for my mental world. I call it Neoland. Sometimes I call it Future Land. Sometimes I call it Pre-Earth. Whatever feels best at that time. That's what it's all about, using verbiage that feels best. Optimizing that verbiage as we progress and as life changes.

Most people, when they visualize, see themselves in the third person doing things. Like watching a movie of their lives. And that's fine for beginners. But if you really want this to work, you need to experience it in the first person. You need to be in the scenario. Looking through your own eyes. Feeling what it feels like. Living it as if it's happening right now.

That's what Neoland is for me. It's not a place I visit. It's a place I live. And the more time I spend there, the more my physical reality starts to match it. Remember back in Chapter 3 when we talked about tuning forks? You're vibrating at the frequency of your future when you're in your mental world. And anything that vibrates at the same frequency naturally pulls toward each other. That's not just a metaphor. That's how this works.

You're All Powerful in Neoland

Here's the best part about your mental world: You're all powerful there. There are no limitations. No bills. No gravity. No physics. No rules except the ones you create.

In Neoland, I have unlimited money. Not a billion dollars. Not a trillion dollars. Whatever number you could possibly come up with, 100 million trillion dollars, I could give that number of dollars to every single person on the planet and still not have scratched the surface of what I have in my mental world. There is no number. It's infinite.

And when I ask people how much money they have in their mental world, they'll say something like ten million dollars. And I say, "That's it?" Surprised. Slightly disappointed. Then they'll up it. "Okay, well, I got ten billion dollars." And I still look at them and say, "That's it?" Eventually they get the point. Stop limiting yourself, even in your imagination. If you're going to dream, dream big. Dream unlimited.

Because here's the thing: When you shoot for 100, you usually end up with 97 or 98. So why not shoot higher? Don't ever tell me the sky's the limit when there are footprints on the moon. You want to know why most people don't manifest big things? Because they don't even allow themselves to imagine big things. They play small even in their own minds.

So in Neoland, go big. Unlimited money. Unlimited success. Unlimited health. Unlimited time. Unlimited freedom. Unlimited everything. Because the bigger you dream in your mental world, the bigger your physical world becomes.

Midnight Till 2 AM

Let me tell you about my routine. Almost every single night, between midnight and 2 AM, I'm in Neoland. Sometimes it goes until 4 or 5 in the morning. My family's asleep. The phone calls and emails have stopped. The world is quiet. And I'm free to live in my future.

And I don't just visualize one scenario. I run multiple scenarios. How would it feel to wake up in my dream house? What would it feel like to check my bank account and see those numbers? How would it feel to walk into a room and have everyone recognize me for the impact I've made on the world? What would it feel like to travel wherever I want, whenever I want, with whoever I want?

I run these scenarios over and over. And the more I do it, the more real they become. The more natural they feel. The more my brain starts to believe they're not just possible but inevitable. And how good it feels. How much I'm enjoying it. Because practice makes perfect. I wasn't able to sit in this headspace for long when I first started. I had to first practice doing this before my body would allow me to sit in this headspace. And before I know it, it's sometimes 4 AM or 5 AM, and I've spent hours living in my future.

If You Can't Stay in a Scenario, Maybe It's Not For You

Here's something important I learned the hard way. If you can't stay in a scenario, sometimes it's because it's not for you.

Sometimes we don't know exactly what we want. So we'll be asking for something that we don't really want. And the universe knows. Your subconscious knows. And it blocks you from staying in that visualization because it's not aligned with who you truly are or where you're truly meant to go.

Let me give you an example. For years, I included club life and VIP sections in my manifestations. I'd visualize myself living that rock star lifestyle, partying in Vegas, bottle service, the whole thing. And yes, I've manifested probably hundreds of VIP sections in my life. But here's the thing: I don't go to clubs like that anymore. Not because I'm high and mighty or need a VIP section everywhere I go. It's because the more success I got, the more money I got, the more popular I grew, the less I yearned to be in those highly populated situations. I thought I wanted that life. But I really didn't.

For years I was manifesting something I didn't truly want deep down. And looking back, there was always resistance. I could never fully sink into those visualizations. My mind would pull me out after a few seconds. I'd be visualizing the club scene and then suddenly I'd be thinking about something completely random. "I need to get milk on the way home." And I'd spend 20 minutes lost in thought tangents before I even realized I'd gotten pulled out of my visualization.

Here's an exact example. I used to visualize a specific scenario with my brother Justice and his best friend Norman. If you've ever seen the video "24K Magic" by Bruno Mars, that's what I was visualizing. Us in Vegas, stunting, dancing down hallways, riding down the Strip in a convertible with the top down. And every single time I'd try to run this scenario, I couldn't get three or four seconds into it before my mind would redirect to something completely different. "I'm thirsty. Where's the water? I left it inside. Let me go get it." And I'd go off into other thought tangents, caught in a mental reel trap, running different scenarios.

This happened over and over for years. And it took me embarrassingly long to finally say, "What if I'm not supposed to be in that exact scenario? Let me change things up. Let me switch the situation and see if I can sit in that version." Because maybe that exact thing isn't meant to happen. Maybe I'm meant to be in a lifestyle that doesn't allow that kind of public freedom.

Think about it. To be Neo Positivity, the voice of the "thoughts become things" movement, changing mankind for the better, having people in companies work together who would never have worked together, getting rid of corruption, changing the world on a massive scale, that would make me larger than Michael Jackson, Oprah Winfrey, and any president that's ever lived, combined. What I aim to do with this world is something that has never been successfully done before. The last person who tried this got hanged on a cross according to the Bible. And it would put me in a situation where hanging out in a casino in Vegas or riding down the strip with the top down, I wouldn't be able to do that. The president can't go anywhere without a motorcade. And I'd be ten times bigger than any president that's ever existed once I complete what I'm looking to do.

So maybe that's why I couldn't visualize it. And when I tweaked the situation in my mind to fit a scenario that aligned better with my actual future, with my brother and Norman in a more private, protected setting where I'm celebrating them in a different way, my brain immediately allowed me to sit in it longer. Longer than I'd ever been able to before.

And here's the kicker: It's no coincidence that once I made that shift, financially, doors opened that I had been waiting to open for years.

So if you're trying to visualize something and you keep getting pulled out, if you can't stay in that scenario no matter how hard you try, ask yourself: Is this really what I want? Or is this what I think I'm supposed to want? Is this aligned with where I'm actually going? Or is this a fantasy that doesn't match my true path?

Sometimes the universe blocks us from manifesting things because deep down, we don't actually want them. And we waste years trying to force something that was never meant for us. So pay attention to the resistance. It might be telling you something important.

Mental Exercises for This Chapter

Here's your mental exercise. And this one's going to require commitment.

Part 1: Build Your Mental World

I want you to create your version of Neoland. Close your eyes. And start building. What does your future look like? Not just the big moments. Everything. Your home. Your bank account. Your relationships. Your daily routine. Your freedom. Your impact. Build it all in your mind. First person. Through your own eyes. Feeling it. Experiencing it. Living it.

And don't limit yourself. In your mental world, there are no rules. Unlimited money. Unlimited time. Unlimited everything. Dream as big as you can possibly dream. And then dream bigger.

Part 2: Live There Daily

Every single day, I want you to spend at least ten minutes in your mental world. Not visualizing. Living. Close your eyes and actually be there. Walk through your dream house. Check your bank account. Feel the freedom. Experience the joy. Live in your future as if it's happening right now. And remember, visualize the boring parts too. The quiet mornings, making breakfast, the simple daily moments that make your brain believe it's real. Stay there for as much of the full ten minutes as you can. And when your ego pulls you out, when it starts throwing evidence that this isn't real, just acknowledge it and go back. Over and over. The more you practice, the longer you'll be able to stay.

Part 3: Spend Your Money in Neoland

Here's a fun one. In your mental world, you have unlimited money. So spend it. Spend as much of it as you can. Buy your dream house. Buy your dream car. Take your family on a trip around the world. Donate to causes you care about. Pay off everyone's debt. Buy buildings. Start businesses. Give it away. Live in the abundance of your mental world. Because the more you experience abundance there, the more it shows up here.

And here's an exercise I've heard over the years that really drives this home. I call it the Orange Card Exercise. Imagine the government gave you an orange card with unlimited money on it. Forever. Anywhere in the world. Unlimited money. But there's one caveat: you can never spend cash again. You can't use physical money, and you can't spend money without this card. Every transaction must go through the orange card.

Would you accept those terms?

Most people say yes immediately. And that reveals something important. Money isn't what's truly important in life. It's the exchange. It's what money represents. It's the freedom, the security, the ability to provide and experience and give.

Now here's what I want you to do. Make a list of everything you would buy if you had that orange card. Everything. Write it all down. And I want you to know, in all the years I've done this exercise with people, I don't know anyone who's written down over 176 things to purchase.

That creates a realization. We think we want unlimited things, unlimited possessions, unlimited toys. But the truth is, there's a limit to what we actually want. And once we realize that, we start to understand what truly makes us happy deep down inside. It's not the objects. It's not the toys. It's the experiences, the freedom, the relationships, the impact, the peace. This exercise opens a window to understanding that money can't buy you everything that matters. And it helps you clarify what you're actually manifesting toward.

So do the exercise. Make the list. And then in your mental world, buy everything on that list. Experience what it feels like to have it all. And then notice what you're still craving. Because that's what you're really after.

Do this every single day. Live in your future. And watch how fast your physical reality starts to match your mental one.

This is proactive manifesting. This is living in your future now. And when you do this consistently, when you spend more time in your mental world than your physical one, your physical world has no choice but to catch up.

CHAPTER TWELVE:
TOKENS AND TRIGGERS
(REMEMBERING TO REMEMBER)

Let me tell you the hardest part of all of this. It's not understanding the concepts. It's not learning the exercises. It's not even believing it works. The hardest part is remembering to do it.

Life comes at you fast. You wake up with the best intentions. You're going to do your affirmations today. You're going to visualize. You're going to spend time in Future Land. You're going to practice feeling the Watcher. You're going to be intentional with your thoughts.

And then your child needs breakfast. Your phone starts buzzing. Your boss emails you. Traffic's a nightmare. Someone cuts you off. Your coworker says something that pisses you off. You get home exhausted. You eat dinner. You zone out in front of the TV. And before you know it, it's bedtime.

And you didn't do a single mental exercise all day.

That's the problem. It's not that you don't want to do the work. It's that you simply forget. You get caught up in life. You get distracted. You go back on autopilot. And autopilot doesn't do mental exercises. Autopilot just reacts to whatever's in front of it.

So the question isn't "Do these exercises work?" The question is, "How do I remember to actually do them?"

And that's where tokens and triggers come in.

What Is a Token?

A token is a physical object that reminds you to wake up. To snap out of autopilot. To do a mental exercise. It's something you carry with you, something you see or feel throughout the day, that triggers you to remember what you're working toward.

For me, it started with a pebble. In the movie The Secret, there's a scene where a man carries a pebble in his pocket. And every time he feels the pebble, he thinks of something he's grateful for. Simple. Powerful. Effective.

So I got a pebble. I put it in my pocket. And every time I felt it, I'd do an affirmation. Or I'd think about something I was manifesting. Or I'd just take a second to be present.

And it worked. For a while. Until I lost the pebble. I don't remember how. It just disappeared one day. And I thought, "Okay, I need something more permanent."

So I switched to a poker chip. I went to Atlantic City to get a fifty dollar poker chip because it was something of value that I wasn't going to lose. It started off as that poker chip from Atlantic City. I didn't write anything on it. And I carried it everywhere. Every time I felt it in my pocket, I'd say thank you. Out loud if I were alone. In my head, if I was around people. It didn't matter what I was thankful for. I'd just say thank you. And that simple act would shift my energy. I still have that poker chip to this day.

Later on, I created my own poker chip that says "Thoughts Become Things, Stay Focused" on one side and "Thank You" on the other side. And it says "Thank You" not for thanking people for purchasing my poker chip, but because it's an easy affirmation to remember. Because most of the times if we do remember to wake ourselves up to do these affirmations, we get fixated on which is the perfect affirmation to do in this moment, what's going on in our life, what do we want to manifest best, what have we been slacking on talking about in affirmations that we should be doing. The next thing you know, we're reminded of that milk we need to pick up on the way home. And that great moment which was supposed to be a great mental exercise turns into nothing more than a brainstorm with no results.

Now I use just my own custom chip. And I hand them out to people I meet. I give them away at my seminars. I leave them places as little reminders. Because if one person finds that chip and it reminds them to think better thoughts, that's a win.

But the point isn't the chip. The point is the reminder. The token is just a tool to help you remember to do the work. Because remembering to remember to do these exercises is the hardest part.

Environmental Triggers

Tokens are great. But they're not the only way to remind yourself to wake up. Environmental triggers are even more powerful. Because they're everywhere. And they're automatic.

What's an environmental trigger? It's any sound, sight, or sensation that you train yourself to respond to with a mental exercise. The token wakes you up to this moment. It is your choice to choose whether you're going to meditate, do a mental exercise like an affirmation, or note something you're thankful for, or proactively manifest a better future scenario.

Every time your phone buzzes, do an affirmation. Ten times. Not just once. These triggers can be used to do an affirmation ten times also, not just once.

Every time you hear a car horn, say thank you.

Every time a dog barks, visualize something you want.

Every time you hear a random beep or chirp in the background, check in with your thoughts.

You get the idea. The world is full of triggers. Beeps. Clicks. Dings. Notifications. Sounds. All of them can be repurposed as reminders to wake up and do the work.

In my speeches, I tell people this all the time. The universe is constantly trying to get your attention. Every little sound, every little interruption, every little moment is the universe saying, "Hey, wake up. Come back. Remember what you're working toward."

But most people treat those sounds as distractions. As annoyances. As things that are getting in the way of their day. And that's a missed opportunity. Because if you reframe those sounds as reminders, suddenly your entire day becomes a series of wake-up calls. And the benefit of these wake-up calls, waking you up to do a mental exercise, is that you would have otherwise spent that time problem solving, which in essence is watering the seed of an issue, thus manifesting more moments where you probably have similar feelings and issues.

Fifty Wake-Up Calls a Day (Because I'm Only Going to Do Ten Percent)

Here's one of my favorite tools. Alarms. Lots of them. I have around 40 alarms set on my phone. And they're all set to vibrate once with a message.

Not a loud ring. Not a song. Just a single vibrate. And when I feel it, I check my phone. And the alarm says something like:

"I deserve this."

"Thank you."

"I expect abundance."

"How would it feel to..."

"I'm so happy and thankful for..."

Simple. Direct. Effective.

Now here's the truth. I don't do all 40 alarms every day. I probably only respond to 6 or 7 of them. Because life happens. I get busy. I get distracted. I'm in a meeting. I'm driving. I'm talking to someone. And I miss the alarm.

But that's okay. Because the point isn't to be perfect. The point is to remind myself as often as possible. And even if I only do 6 or 7 out of 40, that's still 6 or 7 times I woke up and did a mental exercise when I otherwise wouldn't have.

And over time, those 6 or 7 wake-ups add up. They compound. They reprogram your brain. They keep you focused on what you're manifesting instead of getting lost in autopilot. And that number of 6 or 7 that I'm actually getting done will grow. That number will grow double and triple with time, practice, and persistence. Because it won't stay at 6 or 7. If you don't practice, it will and it will even get lower. But if you do, it will grow because you're reshaping and retraining your brain's algorithm to think more of those thoughts throughout the day. You're reprogramming.

Why I Have Fewer Alarms Now

I used to have over 50 alarms. Now I have around 40. You know why? Because my life changed. Some of the things I was manifesting back then, I have now. I don't need as many reminders for those things anymore.

I was manifesting retirement. I'm retired.

I was manifesting financial stability. I have it.

I was manifesting better relationships. I have them.

So I deleted those alarms. And I replaced them with alarms for the new things I'm working on. New goals. New visions. New manifestations.

Your alarms should evolve with you. They're not permanent. They're tools. And when a tool has served its purpose, you put it down and pick up a new one.

How Bad Do You Want It?

Here's the question I ask people when they tell me they don't have time to set alarms or keep track of tokens. How bad do you want it?

Do you want it bad enough to set 10 alarms on your phone? Do you want it bad enough to carry a token in your pocket? Do you want it bad enough to reframe every beep and buzz as a reminder to wake up?

Because if you don't want it that badly, you're not going to get it. Period.

This isn't like a black belt where once you get it it's yours forever. This is more like jogging. You have to work at it consistently to be good at it. This is a lifestyle change. This is a daily practice. This is a commitment. And if you're not willing to commit, you're not going to see the results you want.

I'm not saying you have to be perfect. I'm not saying you have to do every single alarm every single day. But I am saying you have to try. You have to make an effort. You have to prioritize it.

Because the people who actually manifest what they want? They're the ones who set the alarms. They're the ones who carry the tokens. They're the ones who are taking extra steps to wake up more often throughout the day and then do the second step, which is to complete some type of mental exercise and really do it with feeling, not just say words out loud. They're the ones who do the work even when they don't feel like it.

And that's the difference. It's not talent. It's not luck. It's discipline. It's commitment. It's how bad you want it.

Token System

Here's your first mental exercise for this chapter. Get a token. I don't care what it is. A pebble. A coin. A poker chip. A piece of jewelry. A rubber band on your wrist. Anything.

And every time you feel that token throughout the day, do a mental exercise. Say an affirmation. Think of something you're grateful for. Visualize something you're manifesting. Just do something. Anything. As long as it's intentional.

And watch how much more present you become. Watch how much more focused you stay. Watch how many times you wake up throughout the day instead of just sleepwalking through life on autopilot.

Alarms Challenge

Here's your second mental exercise. Set 10 alarms on your phone. Let's start small. Just 10.

Set them at random times throughout the day. Make them vibrate once with a message. And see how many of them you actually respond to.

Don't beat yourself up if you only do 3 or 4 of them. That's 3 or 4 times you woke up when you otherwise wouldn't have. And that's progress.

Do this for a week. And if 10 feels good, add more. If 10 feels like too much, dial it back to 5. The point is to find what works for you. To find a rhythm that keeps you awake without overwhelming you. But remember, if you dial it down to 5, once 5 becomes normal, you need to work your way back up to as many as possible. Because the more time, effort, and energy you spend on this, the better your life will be, the more manifesting you will do, which will make you happier throughout every day.

Environmental Triggers Practice

Here's your third mental exercise for this chapter. Pick one environmental trigger. Just one. Something you hear or see multiple times a day.

Maybe it's your phone buzzing. Maybe it's a car horn. Maybe it's a dog barking. Maybe it's a random beep or chirp you hear in the background. Anything.

And every time that trigger happens, do a quick mental exercise. Say thank you. Say yes. Say I deserve this. Check your thoughts. Anything.

Just train yourself to respond to that trigger with intention instead of reaction. And watch how much that one little habit changes your entire day.

The work isn't hard. The work is remembering to do the work. So set yourself up to remember. Use tokens. Use triggers. Use alarms. Use whatever it takes. Because the universe is constantly trying to wake you up. The question is, are you aware enough? Wake up and do what needs to be done to manifest the life and lifestyle that you want.

CHAPTER THIRTEEN:
COLLECTIVE ENERGY
(AND WHY YOUR FACEBOOK DRAMA
IS KILLING YOUR DREAMS)

Let me tell you something that's going to make you uncomfortable. The people around you are affecting your manifestations. Not just the people you live with. Not just the people you work with. Everyone. Your family. Your friends. Your coworkers. The people you follow on social media. Even the people you barely know who are thinking about you right now.

Their thoughts about you create energy. And that energy hits you whether you realize it or not. And if you're not careful, if you're not intentional about how you handle that energy, it can completely derail everything you're trying to manifest.

Allow me to explain how this works.

Energy Waves (Red, Blue, and White)

Imagine there's an invisible aura around you. It extends about four feet in every direction. And that aura has a color. For this mental image, think of it like a spectrum. Red is the worst, most negative energy. White is a happy neutral. Blue is the greatest, most positive energy. So when you're feeling good, when you're vibrating high, when you're in a positive state, that aura is white or blue. When you're feeling bad, when you're vibrating low, when you're in a negative state, that aura is red.

Now imagine someone thinking about you. Maybe they're worried about you. Maybe they're gossiping about you. Maybe they're mad at you.

Maybe they just heard some bad news about your life and they're sitting there thinking, "Oh, that's so sad."

That thought creates an energy wave. A red wave. And that wave travels through the universe and hits your aura.

If your aura is white, that red wave hits you and turns your aura pink. Not fully red. But not white anymore either. And if enough people are sending you red energy, your aura turns redder and redder. And the redder your aura gets, the harder it is to manifest what you want. Because you're vibrating at a lower frequency.

That's collective energy. That's other people's thoughts affecting your reality. And most people have no idea it's even happening.

1,500 People Thinking "Oh That's So Sad"

Let me give you a real example. Let's say something bad happens in your life. You lose your job. Or you get sick. Or your relationship ends. And you post about it on Facebook.

Now 1,500 people see that post. And most of them think, "Oh, that's so sad. I feel bad for them." And they genuinely do feel bad for you. They're not trying to hurt you. They're trying to be sympathetic.

But what are they actually doing? They're sending you red energy. 1,500 red waves all hitting your aura at the same time. And every time they think about it, today, tomorrow, whenever, every time they think about it, you're getting hit with them. And your aura, which might have been white or blue before, is now dark red. And now you're stuck in that low frequency. And you can't figure out why you feel so heavy. Why you can't shake the sadness. Why everything feels harder than it should.

It's because 1,500 people are holding you in that energy. They're thinking about you as someone who's struggling. Someone who's suffering. Someone who needs sympathy. And the more they think about you that way, the harder it is for you to climb out of it.

That's why I tell people in my seminars and classes, be very careful what you share on social media. Not because you should hide your struggles. But because when you broadcast your struggles to hundreds or thousands of people, you're inviting them to send you low-frequency energy. And that energy has weight. It has power. And it can keep you stuck.

Floyd Mayweather and 50 Cent (Turning Hate Into Fuel)

Now here's the flip side. Some people know how to take that negative energy and transform it into something useful. Floyd Mayweather is a perfect example. That man has haters everywhere. Millions of people who don't like him. Who talk trash about him. Who send him red energy constantly.

But you know what Floyd does? He uses it. He feeds off it. He transforms that red energy into fuel. Because every time someone hates on him, they're also paying attention to him. They're watching his fights. They're buying his pay-per-views. They're talking about him. And that attention turns into dollars.

50 Cent does the same thing. He once said in an interview, "I need my haters so I can use them for energy." He knows that hate is still energy. And if you know how to work with it, you can turn it into fuel.

But most people don't know how to do that. Most people let the red energy hit them and they absorb it. They let it bring them down. They let it affect their mood, their confidence, their manifestations.

So if you're not Floyd Mayweather, if you're not 50 Cent, if you don't know how to transform hate into fuel, then you need to protect yourself from that energy. And that means being intentional about who you let into your space, which often coexists with what you share with the world.

The Pain Body (And How to Starve It Out)

Eckhart Tolle talks about something called the Pain Body. And this concept changed the way I understood energy and relationships forever. This is similar to the ego we talked about in Chapter 6, but where the ego protects your identity, the Pain Body feeds on drama and conflict.

The Pain Body is this entity inside of you that feeds on negative emotions. It feeds on drama. It feeds on conflict. It feeds on sadness, anger, frustration, fear. And when your Pain Body is hungry, it will create situations to feed itself.

Ever notice how some people seem to thrive on drama? How they're always in the middle of some conflict? How they can't go a week without something going wrong? That's their Pain Body. It's hungry, so it's creating drama to feed itself.

And here's the scariest part. Pain Bodies can sense each other. If your Pain Body is hungry, and you're around someone whose Pain Body is also hungry, they're going to find each other. And they're going to start a fight. Not because either of you actually has a problem. But because both Pain Bodies need to eat.

Have you ever had an argument with your spouse where, afterwards, you can't even remember what you were fighting about? That's the Pain Body. It wasn't about the dishes. It wasn't about what they said. It was two Pain Bodies feeding off each other.

And the only way to stop it is to starve it out. To refuse to engage. To refuse to feed the drama. To refuse to give it what it wants.

New Year's Resolution to Never Argue Again

I made a New Year's resolution a few years ago that changed my life. I decided I was never going to argue again. Not with my kids. Not with my friends. Not with strangers on the internet. Not with anyone.

And let me tell you, it was one of the hardest things I've ever done. Because people's Pain Bodies will cause them to attempt to pull you into an argument or attempt to attract your Pain Body. They'll say something that triggers you. They'll push your buttons. They'll bait you. And your Pain Body will scream at you to engage. To defend yourself. To fight back.

But I didn't. I refused. Every single time someone tried to start an argument, I'd just walk away. Or I'd say, "Okay, I hear you," and change the subject. Or I'd just stay silent. Be the bigger person.

And you know what happened? The arguments stopped. Not because people stopped trying. But because I stopped participating. And without my participation, there was no argument. There was just one person yelling into the void.

And the more I did this, the more I starved out my Pain Body. It's not that it got weaker in strength. It's that it lost its appetite. Because we're going to get it on a diet. We're going to starve this Pain Body out to the point where it rarely eats at all. Because it's a part of you. It's not going anywhere, much like the ego. And there's no point in hating it because that's just hating a part of yourself. So we're starving it out. It's just as strong when it does show up, but it shows up less often. The more you starve it out, the more you keep it on that diet of barely any drama per day, the less frequently it appears. And my life became so much more peaceful. So much more calm. So much more aligned with what I was trying to manifest.

Energy Shield Practice

Here's your first mental exercise for this chapter. I want you to visualize your aura. That four-foot bubble around you. And I want you to see it as white. Clean. Pure. Happy neutral.

Now imagine a red energy wave coming toward you. Maybe it's from someone who's worried about you. Maybe it's from someone who's gossiping about you. Maybe it's from someone who's sending you negative thoughts.

As that red wave gets closer to your aura, you have a choice. You can neutralize it, or you can transform it.

To neutralize it, watch the red wave fade to pink as it touches your aura, then to white as it passes through. You're combating the negativity, turning it neutral before it can affect you.

But if you want to take it a step further, like Floyd Mayweather and 50 Cent, you don't just turn it from red to white. You take it past white and turn it blue. That red energy wave, as it gets closer to touching your body, goes from red to white to blue. Blue is the ultimate greatness. Great energy. Pure positivity. At the end of the day, if you're doing this right, you're receiving pure blue positive greatness energy. You're not just protecting yourself. You're transforming negativity into fuel.

Do this visualization every day. And over time, you'll train yourself to automatically transform negative energy instead of absorbing it. You'll stop letting other people's thoughts drag you down. And you'll stay at a high frequency no matter what's happening around you.

Pain Body Diet

Here's your second mental exercise for this chapter. For the next seven days, I want you to starve your Pain Body. That means no drama. No arguments. No conflict. No engaging with negativity.

If someone tries to start an argument, walk away. Be the bigger person. If someone posts something on social media that pisses you off, scroll past it. If your mind starts spiraling into worst-case scenarios, redirect it. If you feel the urge to vent, complain, or gossip, don't.

Just starve it. For seven days. And watch how much lighter you feel. Watch how much clearer your thoughts become. Watch how much easier it is to stay focused on what you're manifesting.

Your Pain Body is going to fight you. It's going to throw everything it can at you to get you to feed it. But if you can make it seven days without feeding it, it won't get weaker in strength, but it will appear less frequently. You're training it to have a smaller appetite. And the less often it shows up, the easier it becomes to stay in a high frequency.

"May He/She Be Well"

Here's your third mental exercise for this chapter, and this one's powerful for your chi.

We all know someone who's struggling in one or more of the four pillars of life: health, wealth, love, and happiness. Whether it be someone's physical body, their mental state, their finances, we all know someone who's going through it.

Anytime you think of someone who's struggling, someone who's sick, someone who's going through a hard time, someone who's suffering, I want you to say this phrase in your mind: "May he be well. May she be well."

Now let me explain what you're actually doing when you feel sympathy for that loved one who's struggling. First, collective energy wise, you're attributing to them experiencing more of this struggle and pain and sadness in the future. Second, you're manifesting a future where you're around people who are struggling. In the spirit of your success, you're supposed to be around people who are more successful than you. Casting or acknowledging a dark cloud over anybody just isn't where you want to be.

The statement itself, "I hope things get better for them" or "I feel so bad this is happening in their life," you're manifesting a future again where you're saying "I feel so bad that this is happening in their life." If you're saying things like "oh I feel so sorry for them," anything you're saying, you're just manifesting the future where you're saying it again.

"May he be well" works because if someone's struggling and you say "Oh, that person's doing great" just as an affirmation to trick your psyche, your ego's going to kick in and say "No, they're not. You're lying." Once again, you're looking at yourself as a liar. The affirmation is giving off a feeling of things you don't want it to give off.

So the most accurate statement you can give in that moment that is in the slightest bit positive is to say "may he be well" because it is accurate. You're not lying. You're not hoping or wishing. You're just putting it out there in a different way. The way it's worded is actually perfect. May he be well, may she be well. You're giving them greatness.

You're basically in a split second envisioning them doing better and you're feeling happy about it. Notice I said feeling happy about it. The feeling is involved in this. When you send out high-frequency energy, you raise your own frequency. And the higher your frequency, the more you attract what you want.

Don't say, "Oh, that's so sad." Don't say, "I feel so bad for them." Don't send them sympathy. Because sympathy is low-frequency energy. It's red energy. And you're not helping them by sending them red energy.

Instead, send them high-frequency energy. Send them the energy of wellness. Of healing. Of things getting better. Say, "May he be well. May she be well." And mean it.

And watch what happens. Not just to them. But to you.

Collective energy is real. Other people's thoughts about you have power. But you don't have to absorb that energy. You don't have to let it drag you down. You can transform it. You can redirect it. You can protect yourself from it. And once you learn how to do that, nothing can stop you from manifesting the life you want.

CHAPTER FOURTEEN:
ON MY DIME, IN GOD/UNIVERSE'S TIME
(WHY DEADLINES KILL YOUR DREAMS)

Let me tell you one of the biggest mistakes people make when they're trying to manifest something. They set a deadline. They say, "I'm going to have this by this date. I'm going to manifest this amount of money by the end of the year. I'm going to meet my person by my birthday. I'm going to get this job by next month."

And you know what happens? The closer the deadline gets, the more doubt creeps in because maybe you've never done anything like that before. The more you start looking around and realizing it's not here yet. The more you start panicking. The more your confidence drops. And the lower your confidence drops, the lower your frequency drops. And the lower your frequency drops, the further away your manifestation gets.

Deadlines can be toxic. They're poison to your manifestation. And I'm going to tell you why, and then I'm going to tell you what to do instead.

Why Deadlines Kill Manifestations

Here's how it works. Let's say you decide you're going to manifest an extra $100,000 by December 31st. It's January 1st right now, so you've got a full year. That feels doable. That feels reasonable. So you start doing the work. You're visualizing. You're affirming. You're staying in a high frequency. Everything's good.

March rolls around. You check your bank account. You've made a little progress. Not $100,000 worth of progress, but some. You're still confident. You're still believing. You're still doing the work.

June rolls around. Halfway through the year. You check your bank account. You're nowhere near $50,000, which is where you should be if you're on track. Now doubt starts creeping in. "Am I doing this right? Is this even working? Maybe I set the goal too high. Maybe I'm not good enough at this."

September rolls around. Three months left. You're maybe at $20,000. You're starting to panic. You're starting to stress. You're starting to wonder if you should just give up. And all of that stress, all of that panic, all of that doubt, it's lowering your frequency. It's pushing your manifestation further away.

December 31st comes. You didn't hit your goal. And now you feel like a failure. You feel like the Law of Attraction doesn't work. You feel like you're not good at this. And you stop doing the work altogether.

That's what deadlines do. They create a ticking clock that breeds doubt, fear, and panic. And all of those emotions are low frequency. And low frequency repels what you want instead of attracting it.

You're Not in Control of the Timing

Here's the truth that nobody wants to hear. You're not in control of the timing. You can control your thoughts. You can control your frequency. You can control your actions. But you can't control when the universe delivers.

The universe has its own timeline. And that timeline is based on things you can't see. Opportunities that haven't presented themselves yet. People who haven't crossed your path yet. Lessons you haven't learned yet. Obstacles that need to be cleared out of the way first.

And when you try to force the universe to work on your timeline, you're fighting against the natural flow. You're creating resistance. And resistance slows everything down.

Just because you made a timeline doesn't mean anyone or anything in the universe has to follow it. And to have the audacity to get mad because it didn't happen in your timeline? Let's say the universe gives you everything you want, and then some, but it gives it to you a year later. For

365 days, you're all sourpuss because you didn't get it in your timeline. That's one of the major reasons why timelines can be toxic.

So instead of setting a deadline, you need to adopt a different mindset. And that mindset is this: On my dime, in God/universe's time.

On My Dime, In God/Universe's Time

Let me explain what this means. "On my dime" means you're putting in the work. You're doing the mental exercises. You're staying in a high frequency. You're taking inspired action. You're investing your energy, your focus, your thoughts into your manifestation. That's your dime. That's your responsibility.

"In God/universe's time" means you're letting go of the timeline. You're trusting that the universe knows when the best time is to deliver what you're asking for. You're surrendering control of the when and just focusing on the what.

And when you do that, when you take the pressure of the deadline off, something magical happens. You relax. You stop stressing. You stop checking your bank account every day to see if the money's there yet. You stop panicking when things don't happen as fast as you want them to. And that relaxation, that trust, that surrender, it raises your frequency. And when your frequency is high, your manifestation comes faster.

I know that sounds backward. But it's true. The less attached you are to the timeline, the faster it shows up.

The Florida Move (And Why I Had to Leave to "Make It")

Let me tell you the story of how I moved to Florida. Because this is the perfect example of how the universe's timing is different from your timing, and how you have to trust the process even when it doesn't make sense.

I was living in New Jersey. I was retired from the police department. I had my pension. Life was great. But I felt stuck. I felt like I was supposed to be somewhere else.

I wasn't trying to leave Jersey until I "made it." Then I was going to buy my Jersey house because it was a five bedroom house sitting on a ton of land and it was beautiful and it was a great living situation. I wasn't trying to leave. And it's not that I needed to make money first. I just needed to "make it" first. I had money.

And one day I entertained the idea: What if I didn't have it backwards? What if I wasn't meant to "make it" and then move to Florida? What if I needed to move to Florida in order to "make it"?

So one day I realized that I could have it backwards. And so mentally I wanted to go over scenarios to see what signs the universe had given me that I may need to be in Florida. And this is where I started to see it. My whole mom's side of the family was in Florida. My best friend since elementary school had moved to Florida a year after we graduated high school. And my dad, who was my other best friend, had just moved to Florida a couple of years before that. And that's when I saw those as signs from the universe that the universe had been giving me for years that I wasn't paying attention to. And that was the big realization.

So I did it. I packed up everything. I moved to Florida. I didn't have anything lined up. Just faith that the universe knew what it was doing.

And within months, my life completely transformed. I started getting opportunities I never would have gotten in New Jersey. I met Elijah Desmond. Started speaking at conferences and things like that more often. And then I won Dentistry's Got Talent, got connected with the entire dental industry. And then my career exploded and is currently expanding in perfect alignment with what I wanted.

But none of that would have happened if I'd stayed in New Jersey waiting for everything to line up perfectly first. I had to follow the signs. I had to trust the timing. I had to move on my dime, on my effort, my energy, and God/universe's time, when the universe saw fit.

How I Got My Pilot's License

And speaking of Florida, let me tell you about the pilot license. Because this is one of my favorite manifestation stories, and it proves that the universe's timing is always perfect.

I've been wanting to be a pilot since before I saw Top Gun. Since I was a child. However, you had to have twenty-twenty vision to be a pilot, which I didn't, so that destroyed that dream for me. I kind of just gave up on it, but it was still in my heart and soul. I knew I was meant to be in the air.

Years later I was a police officer and it was the first really cold day of winter. And I jumped out of my police car to chase someone and it was nighttime and my glasses immediately fogged up. I didn't wear glasses all day, every day. I only wore them when I needed to see faraway lettering, which was very rare after I graduated high school. I barely ever wore my glasses. But for the police department, at nighttime, if you want to see a guy pulling a gun out; you need glasses. So I started wearing them at night in the police department.

So anyway, it's cold out. I jump out of the car and my glasses fog up. I immediately grab them and unfog them, just smear my hands and unfog them real quick. And continue to chase this guy. Less than a second later they're back fogged again. I ripped them off my face, folded them up and put them in my shirt pocket. Continued, caught the guy, arrested him. But I knew something had to change.

Back then laser eye surgery was becoming really popular and I ended up getting it done, which brought being a pilot back into my realm of possibility. So I knew that it would cost $60,000 and as a police officer, maybe saving two to three thousand dollars a year, that would take me forever to save that up. So it was still out of the realm of possibility.

Now, I had manifested $10,000 into my life. And I had never been to the Bahamas before. I had never been on a cruise before. So that was my thing. I was either going to the Bahamas or going on a cruise to the Bahamas. Either way, I was going to the Bahamas. I wasn't going to let anything stop me. That's what I was going to do with a part of this ten grand and the rest I would pay off some bills, splurge a little bit, get some Gucci, I don't know.

Something told me, after the Florida story, after entertaining the idea of maybe I was meant to have done this a long time ago and I just didn't see the signs, just like Florida, I didn't see all the signs. And I said, what else have I been missing out on that I might have been seeing that I haven't been following the signs? And my obsession with flight made me say, what about my pilot's license? I said, let me just call up and see how much it is these days. Mind you, I'm thinking sixty thousand dollars, one hundred percent.

I call up and the lady says, ten thousand dollars.

I started training that Tuesday.

And that's how I got my pilot's license. Not on my timeline. Not when I thought it was going to happen. But on the universe's timeline. When everything aligned perfectly.

If I'd set a deadline, if I'd said I need to get my pilot's license by this date, I would have been trying to force it. I would have been stressed. I would have been in a low frequency. And it probably wouldn't have happened.

But because I focused on "the what" and let go of "the when", the universe delivered it in the most perfect, effortless way possible.

Don't Negotiate with the Universe

Here's another mistake people make. They start out with a big goal. Let's say they want to build a company that makes $10 million in revenue. They visualize it. They feel it. They claim it.

And then doubt creeps in because maybe they've never done anything like that before. And they start negotiating. "Okay, maybe not $10 million. Maybe $5 million. Or you know what, I'd be happy with $1 million. Actually, just a profitable business. That's all I need."

And every time you negotiate down, you're telling the universe, "I don't really believe I can have the big thing. So I'll settle for less."

And the universe says, "Okay, you don't believe you can have it. So you won't."

Don't negotiate with the universe. Remember what we talked about in Chapter 10: Don't ever tell me the sky's the limit when there's footprints on the moon. When you shoot for 100, you usually get 97 or 98. So why not shoot higher?

You can reference Kobe Bryant and Michael Jordan. They both talk about this all the time. You don't negotiate with your goals or your dreams. You set it in stone. You believe it like it already happened. Key emphasis on already happened. Because if it already happened, you wouldn't be negotiating to have less. You'd already have the full amount. You've already had the full thing that you want.

Go big. Claim the big thing. Don't scale it back just because it feels too big.

Remove Deadlines Exercise

Here's your first mental exercise for this chapter. I want you to look at all the goals you're currently working toward. And I want you to remove the deadlines. All of them.

Instead of "I'm going to have this by this date," just say "I have this" or "This is mine."

Instead of "I'm manifesting this amount by the end of the year," just say "I'm manifesting this amount."

Focus on the outcome. Not the timeline. Trust that the universe knows when the perfect time is to deliver it. And let go of the need to control when.

This is going to feel uncomfortable at first. Because we're conditioned to set deadlines. We're conditioned to want everything now. But the discomfort is worth it. Because the second you let go of the deadline, you remove the biggest obstacle standing between you and your manifestation.

And here's something important to note. This is very similar to wanting or desiring having a negative connotation because it's a feeling of lack. It's something that you don't have that you want because you don't have it. And even though drive and wanting and having goals are absolutely necessary to get what you want, there's two sides to every coin, and it does have the negative connotation of lack. The same way with deadlines. Of course you want to have deadlines. It gives you something to shoot for. It makes you work harder, drive, push harder. It makes you do all those things which are great. But it also has a huge negative connotation setback that says once you're nearing the end, the stresses are going to get more, more doubt's going to kick in, more doubt manifests, more doubt manifests more bad.

"On My Dime, In God/Universe's Time"

Here's your second mental exercise for this chapter. Anytime you start feeling impatient, anytime you start stressing about the timing, anytime you start wondering why it's not here yet, I want you to say this phrase: "On my dime, in God/universe's time."

Say it out loud if you can. Or just say it in your head. And let it remind you that your job is to do the work. Your job is to stay in a high frequency. Your job is to keep visualizing, affirming, and believing. But the timing? That's not your job. That's the universe's job.

And when you say that phrase, feel the relief. Feel the weight lift off your shoulders. Feel the trust replace the stress. And watch how much lighter you feel. Watch how much easier it becomes to stay in a high frequency. And watch how much faster your manifestation shows up.

No Negotiation Rule

Here's your third mental exercise for this chapter. Look at your biggest goal. The one that feels almost too big. The one that makes your ego scream, "Who do you think you are?"

And I want you to make a promise to yourself. You're not going to negotiate it down. You're not going to scale it back. You're not going to settle for less just because it feels scary.

You're going to claim it. Fully. Completely. Unapologetically.

And if it feels too big to claim all at once, break it into milestones. Remember back in Chapter 2 when we talked about the basketball player shooting free throws? If they're thinking about the final score, they'll miss. But if they focus on this shot, right now, just this one shot, they make it. And then they focus on the next shot. And the next one. Same principle here. Focus on the next milestone. Then the next one. Then the next one.

But don't give up on the ultimate goal. Because the second you negotiate, you lose. And I don't want you to lose. I want you to win.

On my dime, in God/universe's time. That's the mantra. That's the mindset. That's the key to manifesting without stress, without pressure, without toxic deadlines killing your dreams. Do the work. Trust the timing. And watch the universe deliver in ways you never could have planned.

CHAPTER FIFTEEN:
TRANSFORMING VS OBTAINING

Most people think manifestation is about getting something they don't have. A new car. A new house. More money. A better job. A different life.

And they spend all their time and energy focused on what's missing. On what they don't have. On what they need to obtain.

But that's the problem. Because when you focus on what you don't have, you're operating from a place of lack. And lack attracts more lack.

Here's the truth that changed everything for me: You're not trying to obtain anything. You're trying to transform what you already have.

You already have a car. It might not be the car you want, but it's a car. You already have a house or an apartment. It might not be the one you want, but it's shelter. You already have money. It might not be the amount you want, but it's money.

And when you shift your focus from obtaining to transforming, everything changes. Because now you're operating from a place of abundance. And abundance attracts more abundance.

Let me explain.

God Money Is Already in Your Life

Let me start by explaining what I mean by "God Money." I'm not talking about religion. I'm not talking about anything preachy. I'm talking about a concept that applies to everyone, regardless of what you believe.

Money is an exchange. It's a universal energy that allows us to trade value for value. Whether it's a peso, a ruble, an American dollar, a euro, it doesn't matter. The currency itself is just a symbol. The concept behind it is the same. It's the energy of exchange. And that's what I'm calling God Money.

And here's the key: As long as you have at least one penny to your name, and I mean to your name, including bank accounts, a penny that fell between the cracks of your sofa, anything, God Money is already in your life.

You're not waiting for money to show up. You already have it. It might not be the amount you want. But the energy of it is there. And when you recognize that, when you appreciate that, when you focus on transforming what you already have instead of wishing for what you don't have, that energy expands.

Most people look at the $50 in their bank account and say, "That's not enough. I need more." And all that does is reinforce the feeling of lack. It tells the universe, "I don't have enough." And the universe says, "Okay, you don't have enough. Here's more not enough."

But when you look at that $50 and say, "This is God Money. This is the energy of exchange. And I'm grateful for it. And I'm going to transform this into more," you're operating from abundance. And the universe responds to that.

God Car Is Already in Your Driveway

Same thing with your car. You might be driving a beat up Honda Civic that's 15 years old with dents in the door and a check engine light that's been on for three years.

And you might be visualizing a brand new Tesla. Dreaming about it. Wishing you had it. Feeling frustrated that you don't.

But here's what I want you to understand. That Honda Civic in your driveway? That's also God Car. It's just in a different form, a different shape, a different color. But it's a label that you put on it. "My car." "Her car." "His car." Those are just labels we assign to different forms of the same thing.

You can only occupy one car at a time. So when you're in that Honda Civic, that is God Car. You're in control of it. It's getting you from point A to point B. It's serving its purpose.

And when you recognize that, when you appreciate that, when you stop wishing for a car you don't have and start being grateful for the car you do have, something shifts. You stop operating from lack. You start operating from abundance. And that Honda Civic? It transforms. Maybe you get it detailed. Maybe you fix the dents. Maybe the check engine light miraculously turns off. Or maybe the universe delivers you a better car. But it's not a new car. It's God Car in a different form.

God House Is Where You Live Right Now

Same thing with your house. You might be living in a tiny apartment with thin walls and noisy neighbors. And you might be dreaming about a mansion with a pool and a three-car garage.

But that apartment you're in right now? That's God House. It's just in a different form, a different shape, a different size. But it's a label you put on it. "My house." "Her house." "His house." Those are just labels we assign to shelter.

You can only occupy one house at a time. So when you're in that apartment, that is God House. It's keeping you warm. It's keeping you safe. It's serving its purpose.

And when you recognize that, when you appreciate that, when you stop wishing for a house you don't have and start being grateful for the house you do have, that energy shifts. And that apartment transforms. Or the universe delivers you a bigger house. But it's not a new house. It's God House in a different form.

The 95 Eclipse Story

Let me tell you a story that really drove this home for me.

I had a 1995 Mitsubishi Eclipse. I bought it looking like it was fresh out of the Fast and the Furious movie. And I thought I was the coolest. It made me feel good to have this car.

However, I had two other vehicles that I used primarily, and I only used this car when I was having nights out on the town, which were few and far between. This was when I was heavily into real estate investing and buying up and fixing properties. I was really hands-on, trying to learn carpentry, electrician work, and plumbing on my own. I learned a big lesson during that time: leave it to the pros. Let the pros do what they do. You do what you're great at. That's where you'll get the best results.

Anyway, one day I went to start the Eclipse in my garage after it had been sitting for a while because I was busy buying up properties and fixing them up. The car wouldn't start. The battery was dead. I jumped the battery, got the car started, drove it to the grocery store, and it broke down again. I needed a jump to get home.

This happened one or two more times before I just stopped driving the car. I was doing everything except taking it to a shop and getting it repaired. I got mechanics in my family. I was using their suggestions. Nothing was working.

So I've got this car in my garage. One of my dream cars. Specifically picked it out, hooked it up, and now it's sitting there collecting dust. How can you be appreciative of something that's broken down and collecting dust? It's going to cost a lot of money to get fixed.

And my point at that time was to manifest a bigger, better, faster car. That's progress as humans, right?

So instead of doing what I would have done in the past and what I guess most people would do, ask for a new car, one that works better, one that has fewer problems, one that's reliable, but one that's not currently in my house that I would have to go through the step of getting to my house first, instead of doing that, I realized something.

It's a fool's errand to want a car if you already have one. Because you already have it. It's like asking God for something you already have.

So instead of wanting a new car, hoping for a new car, manifesting a new car, I focused on the one that was currently in my garage.

And what made a lot of sense in this particular situation was that the repairs needed for the car would have cost less than buying a whole new car. So in my mind, I was already a step ahead of the game. If I were to get another 95 Eclipse, an older used car, I would have to buy it, get it there, hope it runs, and if it doesn't, fix it up and get it going.

That's what I was trying to manifest, and that didn't make sense to me because I already had the car there. That was half the battle. More than half the battle. Because that's what most of the money goes toward: getting the car there. Fixing it up to make it run and fixing it up to make it look better, those two things come afterwards. The fact that the car was there meant I was a step ahead of the game.

And so I said, okay, instead of trying to manifest a new God Car, I'm going to recognize that God Car is already in my face, in my garage, and I just need to transform it.

Now, let me tell you, a lot of people might hear this and say that's impossible. But you've got to understand, when you're as deep in the game as me, doing and producing what I'm doing with mental exercises and producing the results I'm producing, you end up shocking yourself like this almost on a daily basis. And that's the one thing I love about it. This is what makes this downright supernatural.

This was a super duper supernatural moment in my life. I am scarred from auto experiences. My first car was a Lincoln Mark VII with a blue ragtop. It would overheat after 35 to 45 minutes of driving. I'd have to pull over at whatever highway I was on, take out the radiator cap, which meant whatever steam and liquid was left over would spew out everywhere, so I had to have some kind of towel or rag. I'd have a gallon of water, pour half of it or all of it into the radiator, and drive for another 35 minutes. I literally did this for a while. If I came out of the house, I would have to fill up the radiator cap first. The car had a leak or other issues; I didn't know what was wrong with it.

And that experience made the 95 Eclipse situation even more frustrating.

So once I wrapped my head around what I needed to do using my manifesting skills and what I know, appreciating the car that I already had sitting in my garage as opposed to asking for a new one, I decided I was going to get it up and running and sell it. I wasn't sure exactly how I was going to do that. I am not a mechanic.

I literally went outside one day after months, after the longest stint of leaving it there untouched, collecting dust. I went out there, tried to start it, and it started right up.

I felt like a god who just manipulated metal with my mind.

Not only did it start up, it started up every time I tried it after that. Which was only two or three times. I put it on the market. A guy shows up, gives me more money than I paid for the car. Zero repairs. Zero physical effort. Lots of mental effort. Make no mistake, every day in my garage, doing the work that I do in my garage, there were mental exercises dedicated to feeling certain things about this 95 Eclipse.

That's the power of transformation. I didn't get a new car. I transformed the car I already had.

The God Garage Story

Here's another example. My garage is my primary workspace when it comes to creating and making speeches. When I'm in my creative process, I'll spend a massive percentage of my time in the garage, rehearsing, performing speeches. A lot of times I just go in the garage and talk for an hour and that becomes my next speech. That's why I'm always recording. So you can see how critical the garage is to what I do as a speaker.

When I moved from New Jersey to Florida, I left a garage that had been a major part of my life and my success for over ten years. I wanted to move to Florida. I wanted a bigger garage, a better garage. I wanted it to look better, so it felt better, so I could produce more in a space that feels better.

But to want a garage that I don't have was a fool's errand. Because all we simply do in life is transform what we currently have. You can only occupy one car at a time. When you get in that car, that is God Car. You're in control of it. When I am in a garage giving a speech, that is God Garage.

146

Regardless of what it looks like and what house it's in, that's just me applying labels to things.

When I'm in a garage, I am in God Garage. So when I went to the next garage, I didn't look at it as a new garage. I looked at it as God Garage that I've already had. It just got upgraded. And I do that for my house. I do that for my bank accounts. I do that for everything.

That's the shift. That's the transformation mindset.

Scarcity to Abundance

When you're constantly looking at what you don't have, you're creating separation. You're creating a feeling of lack. And that feeling of lack keeps you stuck.

But when you shift your focus to what you already have and recognize it as a form of what you want, just in a different shape or size or color, you're operating from abundance. And abundance is magnetic.

Think about it like this. If you have $100 in your bank account and you're constantly thinking, "I need $10,000. I only have $100. That's not enough," what frequency are you vibrating at? Lack. Scarcity. Not enough.

But if you have $100 in your bank account and you think, "I have God Money. This is the energy of exchange. This $100 is proof that money flows to me. And I'm grateful for it. And I'm going to transform this into more," What frequency are you vibrating at? Abundance. Gratitude. More than enough.

Same $100. Different frequency. Different result.

That's what this chapter is about. Recognizing that you already have everything you're trying to manifest. It's just in a different form. And your job isn't to get something new. Your job is to transform what you already have.

Brewster's Millions Exercise

Here's your first mental exercise for this chapter. And this one's fun.

You know the movie Brewster's Millions? Where the guy has to spend $30 million in 30 days or he loses everything? That's what I want you to do. Not in real life. In your imagination. In your mental world.

I want you to spend $10 to $20 million by the end of the day. In your mind. Go wild. And I want you to write down specifics.

Here are some examples: I'm buying a $2 million house in Miami with an ocean view. I'm donating $500,000 to St. Jude's Children's Hospital. I'm buying my mom a $100,000 car. I'm paying off my brother's $50,000 student loans. I'm buying a $3 million vacation home in the Bahamas. I'm investing $1 million in my business. I'm hiring a private chef for $200,000 a year. I'm buying courtside season tickets to the Lakers for $500,000.

Write it all down. Be specific. And feel what it feels like to spend that money. Feel the abundance. Feel the generosity. Feel the freedom.

And when you're done, you'll realize something. You just spent $10 to $20 million. In your mind. And it felt good. And your brain doesn't know the difference between what you vividly imagined and what you actually experienced. So you just sent out the frequency of someone who has $10 to $20 million to spend. And the universe is going to respond to that frequency.

Lifetime Gross Earnings

Here's your second mental exercise for this chapter. I want you to add up your lifetime gross earnings. Everything you've ever made in your entire life. All the way back to your first job at McDonald's. All the way up to today.

Every paycheck. Every side hustle. Every gift. Every dollar. Add it all up.

Note: This exercise is most effective and impactful for those whose lifetime gross earnings exceed $1 million. If your total is less than that, that's okay. The principle still applies. Just work with whatever your total is.

Now here's what I want you to do. Look at that number. Let's say it's $600,000. Or $800,000. Or $1.2 million. Whatever it is.

And I want you to feel proud of that. I want you to recognize that you've earned that. You've created that. You've brought that into your life.

And then I want you to do something that's going to trick your psyche. I want you to tell yourself that you manifested that entire amount last night. All of it. In one night. You woke up this morning and that entire amount was in your account.

How does that feel? How does it feel to have manifested $600,000 overnight? Or $1.2 million overnight?

That's abundance. That's the frequency you want to stay in. Because you did manifest that amount. It just took you longer than one night. But the energy is the same. The achievement is the same. And when you feel that achievement, when you feel that abundance, you attract more of it.

Mental Exercise for This Chapter

Here's your third mental exercise for this chapter. Pick one thing in your life that you're unhappy with. Your car. Your house. Your bank account. Your job. Whatever.

And instead of wishing for something different, I want you to spend the next seven days being grateful for what you already have. Recognize it as God Car, God House, God Money, God Job. Recognize that it's already the thing you want, just in a different form.

And watch what happens. Watch how it starts to transform. Not because you're wishing for something new. But because you're appreciating what you already have. And appreciation is the highest frequency there is.

You're not trying to obtain anything. You're trying to transform what you already have. And when you make that shift, when you move from scarcity to abundance, from lack to gratitude, from wishing to appreciating, everything changes. Because you're no longer waiting for the universe to give you something. You're recognizing that the universe has already given it to you. And all you have to do is to transform it.

CHAPTER SIXTEEN:
MONEY BLOCKS
(AND HOW TO FINALLY BREAK THROUGH THEM)

I'm going to be honest with you. Money is the hardest thing to manifest. It just is. I can manifest free things all day long. I can manifest opportunities. I can manifest connections. I can manifest experiences. But money? That's where most people, including me, hit a wall. And I'm still dealing with it and working my way through it.

And there's a reason for that. Money blocks run deep. Deeper than almost anything else. Because money is tied to survival. It's tied to your childhood. It's tied to your parents' beliefs. It's tied to your self-worth. It's tied to guilt, shame, fear, and a whole bunch of other emotions that you probably don't even realize are there.

So if you're struggling to manifest money, you're not alone. And you're not broken. You just have some blocks that need to be cleared. And in this chapter, I'm going to show you how to identify them and break through them.

Your Relationship with Money

In my seminars, I ask people to clear their minds and then think about the essence of money. The currency transfer. All that money stands for, whether it be a peso or a dollar. I want them to think of what I call God Money, the essence of what money stands for, what it does, what its active role is in our lives and how it's used. Take that essence as a whole and then I tell them to put a face to it. Friend, foe, celebrity, anyone on earth. Just put a face to it. What's the first face that pops up?

For some people, it's their father's face. Maybe their dad was always stressed about money. Always working. Always worried about bills. And now, when they think about money, they see his stressed-out face. And that creates a subconscious association: money equals stress.

For some people, it's a rich person they know. Maybe someone who was wealthy but miserable. Or someone who was wealthy and arrogant. And now, when they think about money, they see that person's face. And that creates an association: money equals being a jerk.

When I first tried this exercise, the face that popped in my mind was the Rock, Dwayne Johnson. And I had to analyze why that face, and I want you to do the same. When I think about The Rock, I think about respect. I think about power. I think about someone who's accomplished, disciplined, and successful. But also someone who's still a little bit out of reach. Someone I admire. Someone I respect. Someone I know I'll eventually link up with, but we're not quite there yet.

That's my relationship with money. Respectful. Aspirational. And confident that we'll eventually be close.

But for a lot of people, when they think about money, they see something negative. Something stressful. Something shameful. Something that makes them uncomfortable. And that's the block. That's what's keeping them from manifesting it.

So the first step to breaking through your money blocks is to identify what face you see. And if it's a negative face, you need to change it. You need to reprogram your brain to associate money with something positive, something powerful, something you actually want to be around.

Money Honey (Your Spouse)

Here's a concept that I learned from an elderly man in New York that helped me transform my relationship with money. I started treating money like a spouse. And I call it Money Honey.

Imagine money is your romantic partner. How do you talk to your partner? How do you treat them? Do you insult them? Do you push them away? Do you act like you don't need them?

No. You treat them with respect. You appreciate them. You make them feel valued. You show them love. You tell them you want them around.

So why don't we do that with money?

Most people talk about money like it's the enemy. "I hate dealing with money. Money is so stressful. I never have enough money. Money is the root of all evil." And then they wonder why money doesn't stick around.

If you talked to your spouse the way you talk about money, they'd leave you. So stop insulting money. Stop pushing it away. Start treating it like someone you love. Someone you appreciate. Someone you want in your life.

Here's how I do it. When I'm about to make a purchase, let's say my wife wants to buy a $1,400 purse, and I start to hesitate, I imagine Money Honey laughing at me, saying, "Don't insult me. I don't have limits. You can have whatever you want. I love you. You can have anything you want, your heart's desire. If you hesitate, that means you're thinking that I have limits and I don't." That's what Money Honey is saying to you.

And that shift in perspective changes everything. I'm not thinking about scarcity anymore. I'm thinking about abundance. I'm thinking about money as something that's on my side, not something I'm fighting against.

Try it. Next time you're hesitating to spend money on something you want, imagine Money Honey saying those words to you. And see how that changes the way you feel about the purchase.

The Orange Card Test

Here's a thought experiment that's going to mess with your head. This came to me during meditation, and it completely shifted the way I think about money.

Imagine I hand you an orange card. And I tell you that this card has unlimited funds on it. You can buy anything you want. Anywhere. Anytime. No limit.

But there's one rule. You can never use cash again. Ever. For the rest of your life, you can only use this orange card.

Would you take it?

Most people say yes immediately. But as they think about it, they start to realize that money's not actually what they want at all.

They want the house. The car. The food. The experiences. The security. The freedom. But they don't want the money itself. Because money is just a tool. It's just a means to an end. Instead of giving you the money to buy the car, what if I gave you the car? Instead of giving you the money to buy the house or the gas, what if I just gave it to you? Would you be equally happy? The answer ends up being yes. And people who do have money sitting in a safe or bank account for months doing nothing realize the cash isn't what they want. It's what they can exchange the cash for.

And once you realize that, once you understand that money is not the goal, it's just the vehicle, you stop obsessing over the money and you start focusing on what you actually want.

Do you want money? Or do you want the lifestyle money provides?

Do you want money? Or do you want the freedom money provides?

Do you want money? Or do you want the security money provides?

Figure out what you actually want. And then manifest that. Because when you focus on the end result instead of the money, the money shows up a lot easier. You need to see it this way if you're going to succeed in these practices.

"I Love Money"

Here's one of the most powerful affirmations I've ever used. And it's simple. Just three words.

"I love money."

That's it. Say it out loud right now. "I love money."

Does it feel weird? Does it feel uncomfortable? Does it feel wrong?

If yes, that's your block. That's the resistance. That's your current thought process based on your training and experiences that says wanting money is greedy, or selfish, or bad.

But here's the truth. Money is neutral. It's not good or bad. It's just energy. It's just a tool. And the more of it you have, the more good you can do in the world.

You can't help people if you're broke. You can't donate to causes you care about if you're struggling to pay your own bills. You can't take care of your family if you're constantly stressed about money.

So stop feeling guilty about wanting money. Stop apologizing for it. And start loving it.

Say it every single day. "I love money." Say it until the discomfort goes away. Say it until it feels true. Say it until your brain starts believing it.

Because the more you love money, the more money loves you back. And the more money loves you back, the more it shows up in your life.

I Struggled with Money Blocks Too

Let me be real with you. I have struggled with many types of money blocks in my life, and I've done a lot of work to get through a lot of them. But the fact that I'm not a billionaire clearly means there are money blocks still lingering that I'm still dealing with. There may always be some kind of money block. This isn't an absolute practice. But this is one of the biggest wishes people have.

Have I gotten through the money blocks I have? A large percentage of them, yes. Do I have a lot of work to do? Yes. We are all works in progress and that's what it'll be. In this entire book, we are works in progress and we will be that until the day we die.

I had beliefs from my childhood. Beliefs from growing up broke. Beliefs from watching my family struggle. Beliefs from society telling me that wanting money was greedy. All of that was buried in my subconscious, creating resistance.

155

But then I started doing the work. I started identifying the blocks. I started reframing my relationship with money. I started using the exercises I'm teaching you in this chapter. And things started to shift.

And now? I'm in a completely different tax bracket than I was a few years ago. Not because I got lucky. Not because I stumbled into something. Because I broke through many of my money blocks and opened myself up to receive.

So if you're struggling with money, I get it. I've been there and I'm still working through it. But I'm also here to tell you that it's possible to break through. You just have to be willing to do the uncomfortable work of looking at your blocks, acknowledging them, and reprogramming them. Honestly, I can't say I've conquered my money blocks and I'm not a gazillionaire.

Your Money Association

Here's your first mental exercise for this chapter. Close your eyes. Think about money. And notice what face pops up.

Whose face is it? What does that person represent to you? What emotions come up when you see that face?

If it's a positive face, someone you admire, someone you respect, someone who represents abundance, great. Keep that association.

But if it's a negative face, someone who was stressed, someone who was greedy, someone who represents struggle, you need to change it.

Pick a new face. Someone who represents the kind of relationship you want to have with money. Someone who's wealthy but also happy. Someone who's successful but also generous. Someone you look up to.

For me right now, it's The Rock. For now, I'm choosing to keep it there. For you, it might be someone else. It doesn't matter who it is. Just pick someone who makes you feel good when you think about money.

And every time you think about money from now on, bring that face to mind. Reprogram the association. Train your brain to link money with something positive instead of something negative.

Money Honey Practice

Here's your second mental exercise for this chapter. Start treating money like your spouse. Talk to it. Appreciate it. Show it love.

Every time you receive money, whether it's a paycheck, a refund, a gift, whatever, say thank you. Out loud if you can. "Thank you, Money Honey. I appreciate you. I'm so glad you're here."

Every time you spend money, say, "Thank you for allowing me to have this. Thank you for flowing through my life."

And when you're hesitating to spend money on something you actually want, imagine Money Honey saying, "Don't insult me. I don't have limits. Get it."

This might feel silly at first. But I promise you, if you do this consistently, your relationship with money will transform. And when your relationship with money transforms, your ability to attract it transforms too.

"I Love Money"

Here's your third mental exercise for this chapter. Say this affirmation ten times a day, every single day, for the next 30 days: "I love money."

Say it out loud. Say it with conviction. Say it until the discomfort goes away. Say it until it feels true.

And if you want to take it a step further, add a reason. "I love money because it allows me to take care of my family." "I love money because it gives me freedom." "I love money because I can use it to help people."

The more you say it, the more your brain starts to believe it. And the more your brain believes it, the more money starts showing up in your life.

Money blocks are real. They run deep. And they're probably the biggest obstacle standing between you and the financial abundance you want. But they're not permanent. They can be identified and reprogrammed. Then they can be cleared. And once you do that, once you break through those blocks, money starts flowing to you in ways you never thought possible. So do the work. Face the blocks. And watch what happens.

CHAPTER SEVENTEEN:
TAKING INSPIRED ACTION
(EVEN IF IT'S JUST MINDSET TRAINING)

Let me tell you something that's going to save you years of frustration. The Law of Attraction is not about sitting on your couch visualizing your dream life and then waiting for it to magically appear at your doorstep. That's not how this works. And anyone who tells you that's how it works is lying to you.

Yes, you need to do the mental work. Yes, you need to visualize. Yes, you need to affirm. And yes, you need to stay in a high frequency. But you also need to do something that most Law of Attraction teachers don't talk about enough. You need to take action. Not just any action. Inspired action.

And here's the difference. Regular action is when you force yourself to do something because you think you're supposed to. You're grinding. You're hustling. You're pushing. And it feels heavy. It feels hard. It feels like work.

Inspired action is when something pulls you forward. When an idea hits you and you can't stop thinking about it. When an opportunity shows up and you just know you're supposed to say yes. When you feel compelled to reach out to someone, go somewhere, do something, even if it doesn't make logical sense. That's inspired action. And by miracles, I mean success, whether it be in health, wealth, love, or happiness. All the above. That's what creates miracles.

Now, taking inspired action doesn't always have to be getting up and going to a conference, making a phone call, or writing an email. Taking inspired action could be trusting your gut, going to a quiet place, making sure the house is cleared out with no noises, and then actually meditating for half an hour every day until it comes into your life. That's an action.

That's a thing. It's about trusting your gut and becoming in perfect alignment with what you want, then manifesting that into your reality as your new life and lifestyle.

Get Out of Your Comfort Zone

Here's the truth. Your manifestation is not going to show up in your living room while you're watching TV, scrolling on your phone, your tablet, or your computer. It's going to show up when you put yourself in situations where it can find you.

You want to manifest a new job? You've got to go to networking events. You've got to meet people. You've got to put yourself out there.

You want to manifest a relationship? You've got to leave your house. You've got to go places where you might meet someone. You've got to be open to conversations with strangers.

You want to manifest financial abundance? You've got to invest in yourself. You've got to spend money on things that scare you. You've got to take risks.

Because here's the thing. Your comfort zone is keeping you safe. But it's also keeping you stuck. And if you want your life to change, you've got to be willing to step outside of what's comfortable and into what's possible.

And I'm not saying you have to do something crazy. I'm not saying you have to quit your job tomorrow and move to another country. I'm saying you have to do things that push you just a little bit outside of where you are right now.

Because that's where the magic happens. That's where the opportunities are. That's where the universe can actually reach you.

How I Lost 69 Pounds: Inspired Action Isn't Always External

Remember, taking inspired action doesn't always mean going to conferences or networking events. Sometimes inspired action is trusting your gut to do the internal work—the mental exercises, the meditation, the daily commitment to changing your thoughts.

Let me tell you exactly how I lost 69 pounds without exercising once. This is the full story I teased back in Chapter 2, and now you have all the tools to understand how I actually did it.

I went from 264 pounds to 195. That's 69 pounds. And I didn't work out. Not once. The injuries from being a cop—both ankles, both knees, both wrists, both shoulders, my spine—they're still there. Exercise wasn't an option.

So I had to manifest weight loss purely through mental work. And I did it publicly on Facebook so people could watch.

Here's what I actually did every single day, using the techniques you now know from earlier chapters:

The Core Belief (Chapter 2: Thought Foundations) I built my entire approach on this foundation: There is no food, no molecule, nothing on Earth that can make a person fat—except the belief that what you're eating is making you fat. If you believe food makes you fat, it will. If you believe your body knows how to process it, that's what happens.

That became my unshakable thought foundation. Everything else sat on top of that.

Lofty Questions (Chapter 9: Affirmations) While eating my daily cheeseburger or cheesesteak—yes, every single day—I'd ask myself lofty questions:

- "Why does my body process food so efficiently?"
- "Why am I so good at burning fat?"
- "Why do I feel so healthy and energized?"

These bypassed my ego completely. My subconscious started generating answers automatically.

The Knot in Your Chest Test (Chapter 9) I tested every affirmation. "I'm skinny" dropped the knot—my ego knew it was a lie. But "I'm so happy and thankful that I'm losing weight" raised the knot. That one was true. I could feel it. So I used that one.

Compound Exercises (Chapter 10: All Four Layers) I didn't just think about being thin. I stacked all four layers:

- Mental: Visualized myself at 195, wearing clothes that fit better
- Emotional: Felt what it was like to be lighter, more energetic, confident
- Physical: Noticed how my body felt while eating—satisfied, fueled, not guilty
- Spiritual: The Watcher watching me eat, knowing I was transforming my body

Visualizing the Boring Parts (Chapter 10) I didn't just visualize the highlight reel of being thin. I visualized boring moments: walking up stairs without being winded, bending down to tie my shoes easily, sitting in a chair without it creaking, shopping for regular-sized clothes. Those boring moments made my brain believe I'd already been there.

Tokens and Alarms (Chapter 12: Remembering to Remember) I set alarms throughout the day—especially around meal times. Every time I ate, I'd do a quick mental exercise. Feel gratitude. Check my thoughts. Remind myself of my foundation belief.

Proactive Manifesting (Chapter 11: Living in Your Future) I spent time in Neoland seeing myself at 195. Not watching myself from the outside like a movie. First-person. Through my own eyes. Feeling it. Living it. Hours some nights, visualizing my future body as my current reality.

Environmental Triggers (Chapter 12) Every time I saw food, instead of thinking "this will make me fat," I'd use it as a trigger to think "my body knows exactly what to do with this." TV commercials for fast food? Trigger. Passing a restaurant? Trigger. Opening the fridge? Trigger.

Transforming vs Obtaining (Chapter 15) I wasn't trying to obtain a new body. I was transforming the body I already had. God Body was already mine—I was just changing its form. That shift from lack to abundance changed everything.

The Inspired Action Part. Here's where the inspired action comes in: I felt pulled to do this publicly on Facebook. My ego screamed, "Don't do that! What if you fail? What if people judge you?"

But something told me to do it, anyway. So I posted updates. Pictures. Videos of me eating cheeseburgers and cheesesteaks. Weight loss progress every week.

And you know what happened? People watched. They commented. They supported. And that public accountability became fuel. Their positive energy (blue waves from Chapter 13) hit my aura and raised my frequency even higher.

The world watched me drop from 264 to 195 while eating foods that "shouldn't" allow that to happen. That's what gained me my first big Facebook following. People wanted to know how.

Belief Over Logic My ego fought me hard at first. Logic says you can't eat cheeseburgers every day and lose weight. But I wasn't operating on logic. I was operating on belief. And belief backed by consistent mental exercises is stronger than logic every single time.

Years later, after I'd already lost all the weight and maintained 195, I learned about dendrites (Chapter 2). That's when I understood why it worked on a neurological level. And that's when I trained myself to drive past my favorite cheesesteak spot without even a craving. Just neutral. Like it wasn't even there.

The Point? Inspired action isn't always external. Sometimes it's the discipline to do your mental exercises every single day. Sometimes it's trusting your gut to try something that defies logic. Sometimes it's the courage to do it publicly when your ego tells you to hide.

I lost 69 pounds without a single workout. Just mental work. Daily commitment. Stacking every technique in this book. That's inspired action too.

Now let me tell you about the external inspired action that changed my life when I moved to Tampa...

Taking Tampa by Storm

Let me tell you what I did when I first moved to Tampa. I didn't know anyone. I didn't have any connections. I was starting from scratch.

And most people in that situation would stay home. They'd wait for things to happen. They'd send out resumes online and hope for the best.

But I didn't do that. I went to 23 networking events in the first month. Twenty-three. Some of them were free. Some of them cost money. But I went to all of them.

And at first, it was uncomfortable. I didn't know anyone. I didn't know what to say. I felt out of place. But I kept showing up. I kept introducing myself. I kept having conversations. I kept handing out my contact information.

And you know what happened? People started to know who I was. They started recognizing me. They started introducing me to other people. And within a few months, I went from knowing nobody to a point where they didn't all know me, but I felt like I knew everybody. I felt like I could reach anyone in Tampa in just two or three phone calls. I went from knowing nobody to being connected to some of the most influential people in Tampa.

That didn't happen because I sat at home visualizing it. It happened because I put myself in rooms where it could happen. That's inspired action.

BNI, Gary, and Podfest

Let me tell you one of my favorite manifestation stories. Because this is proof that inspired action creates opportunities you could never plan for.

164

I was leaving a BNI chapter meeting, and as I was leaving, one of the guys in the chapter named Gary came running out to catch me before I left. And he told me about this event called Podfest that they have every year. And he said, since I have a podcast, I should go. And my initial thought was, why would I go pay to sit in a room with a bunch of my competitors? But I had that feeling, that tingling spider sense type feeling, that I should go. And I asked him when it was, and he said, "Well, you should go next year because it starts tomorrow. And I know it's last minute and everybody's got a family and finances and things to do."

And I told Gary, "I'm more of a now type person. I came to Tampa for a reason. And it's not to wait for next year. So I'm going."

And he was pleased. He said, "Cool. I will talk to my friend who's the owner. His name is Chris. And I'll get you a discount code."

And I was excited. I had never been to a conference before. And when he said the thing about the coupon code, I thought to myself, oh, I have to pay for this. Alright, well, let's see how much it is. So I go to their website. It's $500. And this made me say no. Immediately I said no, I'm not paying $500 to sit in a room full of my competitors. Why would they bring me business? They're my competitors. Why would I bring them business? They're my competitors. So it just didn't make sense to me.

But the universe was saying, go. This is why you moved to Florida. And as much as I said, maybe it's not this, maybe this is the next opportunity, I kept feeling pulled. Because I'm not used to dealing with money for events. For years I've operated off the thought process of: if you really want me there, you will give me a ticket. If the universe really wants me there, it will prompt you in your mind to give me a ticket. And I'd been doing it for over 15 years before that. And it worked out amazingly. Why would I change it? Well, if you want something new, you have to try something new.

So I was looking forward to the coupon code. I was looking forward to the coupon code saying zero dollars after I entered it. So I entered the coupon code. And the price dropped down to a whopping $494.

And then I really said no. I said, forget this. How badly does this guy want me there? He's going to give me $6 off? That was a slap in the face to me. That's how I felt at the time.

However, the universe was still nudging me. And I was at the biggest point in my life of listening to those nudges and gaining from them.

So right when I'm saying no to $494 and in my mind upset at this owner of Podfest that I'd never met and didn't even know what he looked like at the time, my phone rings. And it's Gary. And he says, "Hey, I have to pass by your neck of the woods to get there. I have to drive right past you to get there. Would you like to carpool?"

I said to myself, this is how the universe has been working when it's been hand delivering me my manifestations. I said, you know what? I'm going. I got the money. The money was never the problem. It's $500, that's nothing. I was getting paid that for an hour or less of speaking, easy. But I said yes, I'll go.

Gary calls me back 10 minutes later and says, "Hey, they just upgraded my suite. Got big bedrooms and all this other stuff. Why don't you stay with me and save money on a hotel?"

And I said, man, this is exactly how my manifestations usually go. And so I went. I ended up going. And he introduced me to Chris.

Elijah and the Tour Bus to Dykema

At Podfest is where I met Elijah. I was in Nashville speaking for Elijah and a company called On Diem. The owner is Joe Fogg, Elijah's good friend. And I was looking to get deeper into the dental world.

When I met Elijah at Podfest, he told me about the high suicide and depression rates in the dental industry. And he said that my message, the way I put it out there, could really change the dental industry as a whole, the entire industry. And I looked forward to the challenge. I like making moves that affect the globe as opposed to just my state. So I started speaking in the dental world.

After the speaking gigs, the conference was almost done. We were at the resort or hotel pool, a whole group of us. And I had a moment with Elijah where I asked him, "Okay, if you were me, what would you do next?"

And he said, "Just keep showing up. You're doing amazing. You're rocking the industry. You're making a big splash. Everyone loves you. Just keep showing up."

And to me, I'm just thinking, yeah, cool, but what next?

And he said, "Dykema's the next conference."

And I said, "When is that?"

He said, "It's in a couple days."

Now, at this point, I have two checked luggages and a flight home the next day. And so I told him, "I have two checked bags and a flight home the next day. I can't just change it."

And he kind of gave me a look of "how bad do you want it?" Which is something I say a lot to people in my speeches and seminars when referencing the Law of Attraction, taking inspired action, and changing your future.

So I thought to myself, what would it look like to cancel my flight home and go to Dykema? I started doing the math in my head. The flight from Nashville to Dykema. The hotel at Dykema. All types of different things, running scenarios. And I wanted to go. I wanted to make this happen.

The major blockade was my father. When you go back to even me in the police department, my father would not watch my kids for me if I was taking off of work for fun. He would only watch the kids if it were for me to go to work. It was a thing. I'm not saying it was unanimous every time, but that was his thing. If he were watching the kids so I could go to Atlantic City or go hang out at the bar with my friends, he wouldn't do it. It was only for work.

So I called my dad. I said, "Hey, I had this opportunity to go to this conference called Dykema. I need you to watch the kids for another three or four days so I can go there and do my thing, meet people, network, blah blah blah."

Expecting resistance from him, he says, "Yeah, go. Do your thing. That's what you're down there for."

At that moment, it was like the sun shone on me and I knew what I needed to do. So I called Elijah. I said, "I'm in."

And he mentioned something to me that I had totally forgotten about. Something that existed in the background, creeping, that I totally forgot about. The entry fee. It cost almost $1,000 to get into the conference. Plus the flight and the hotel.

Elijah tells me this, and this is like the universe saying, no matter what you want, no matter what you ask for, the universe will show you, if not prove to you, that you cannot have it. And how you respond to that determines if and when you get it.

When Elijah said that the ticket was basically almost a thousand dollars, that was the universe kicking me in my stomach saying you can't have it. And you know what I said? I got the money. It's not about the money. I had the money. I didn't want to spend it. Not on that. But I had it. And the universe was calling me. So what did I do?

I said, "Cool." I hung up the phone. I accepted my fate. This was my future and it was going to cost me a thousand dollars. I'll take it. So I packed my bags, got ready to leave.

And Elijah says, "Hey, you remember that tour bus that we've been taking around the country?"

And I said, "Yeah, you've been going from conference to conference, spreading information about your conferences and events."

And he says, "Yes, our tour bus leaves in the morning to Dykema. Why don't you come with us?"

And once again, just like with Gary, my transportation is lined up.

"While we're there, got an extra bed on the tour bus. Why don't you just stay there?"

Once again, just like with Gary, my room and board is lined up. Now the universe is really starting to conspire in my favor, just like with

Podfest, and I'm loving it. There's just one more thing. That damn thousand dollar entry fee.

So the next morning I get down to the lobby and Elijah's on the phone. Everybody's got their backpacks. The tour bus is pulling up. Elijah's on the phone. He hangs up the phone. He says, "I just got done talking to the owner of Dykema. He loves you. He loves your content, what you're all about. He's gonna comp you a ticket."

And that right there is one of the moments, one of the many moments that are almost daily, where I think to myself, this is freaky how I'm doing this. It makes no sense how I'm doing this. But I love it. I have a formula. It works. And I'm going to keep honing it, making it better, keep using it to make my life more fun and better.

Greater NY Dental (Alone and Confident)

Let me tell you another story that proves inspired action works. I was supposed to go to the Greater New York Dental Meeting with Elijah. But two days before the event, he tested positive for COVID. He couldn't go. And I was left with a decision. Do I go alone? Or do I skip it?

And my ego was screaming at me to skip it. "You don't know anyone there. You're going to feel out of place. You're going to look stupid."

But something in me said, "Go anyway."

So I went. Alone. To one of the biggest dental conferences in the world. And I didn't know a single person there.

And I remember walking through the convention center, surrounded by thousands of dental professionals, thinking, "I'm just gonna law of attraction this shit."

That was my mindset. I'm here. I showed up. The universe put me here for a reason. So I'm just going to trust that.

And you know what happened? A woman walked up to me and said, "I love your shirt." If you see me in a shirt, almost every shirt I wear says "Thoughts Become Things" unless I'm in a suit. And we started talking.

And she introduced me to someone else. And that person introduced me to someone else. And before I knew it, I was connected.

I didn't hide in the corner. I didn't sit in my hotel room. I walked around like I owned the place. Like I belonged there. Like I was supposed to be there. And people responded to that energy.

That's inspired action. That's showing up even when you're nervous. That's trusting the process. That's acting like you've been there before, even when you haven't.

Smart Tips for Growth

Let me give you some principles that have been critical to my growth. These aren't just stories. These are practices I live by…

If You're the Smartest Person in the Room, Change Rooms

It's something I've heard repeatedly over the years, and it's one of the best pieces of advice I've ever received. If you're the smartest person in the room, you're in the wrong room.

Because growth doesn't happen when you're comfortable. Growth doesn't happen when you're the expert. Growth happens when you're challenged. When you're learning. When you're around people who know more than you, who've done more than you, who've achieved more than you.

So if you want to level up, you've got to put yourself in rooms where you're the least experienced person. Where you're the rookie. Where you're the one asking questions instead of answering them.

And that's uncomfortable. Your ego doesn't like it. Your ego wants to be the expert. Your ego wants to be the one people look up to.

But your ego is also the thing keeping you stuck. So ignore it. Get in rooms where you don't belong yet. And watch how fast you grow.

Act Like You've Been There Before

Here's something my father drilled into me growing up. He never let me celebrate after scoring. That was one of his biggest things about scoring a point or a touchdown. Act like you've been there before. And that advice has been detrimental to my success, my confidence, my vibe, all of the above.

When you walk into a room, any room, act like you've been there before.

Don't be starstruck. Don't be overly impressed. Don't act like you don't belong. Act like you've been in rooms like this a hundred times. Act like you're comfortable. Act like you're confident.

Not in an arrogant way. Not in a cocky way. Just in a calm, collected, "I belong here" kind of way.

Because when you act like you belong, people treat you like you belong. When you act like you're important, people treat you like you're important. When you act like you're successful, people respond to you as if you're successful.

That's not fake it till you make it. That's confidence. That's knowing your worth. That's refusing to shrink yourself just because you're in a room with people who've achieved more than you.

And the more you practice this, the more natural it becomes. Until one day, you're not acting anymore. You actually do belong. You actually are successful. You actually have achieved everything you set out to achieve.

But it starts with acting like it's already true. Even when it's not. Yet.

The Rocket Booster Analogy

Let me talk about something that's hard but necessary. Not everyone who's in your life right now is supposed to stay in your life forever. Some people are only meant to be with you for a season. For a chapter. For a specific part of your journey.

And when that chapter ends, you've got to let them go.

I call it the rocket booster analogy. When a rocket launches into space, it has boosters attached to it. Those boosters give it the power it needs to get off the ground. But once the rocket gets high enough, those boosters fall away. Because they're not needed anymore. And if they stayed attached, they'd actually slow the rocket down.

Some people in your life are rocket boosters. They helped you get where you are. They supported you. They believed in you. And you'll always be grateful for your time together. And you need to be grateful for your time together. Because a lot of my memories growing up are with one specific person who I called my best friend for most of my life. And it sucks that, I mean, we have such a great time when we're together reminiscing. And it sucks that I kind of had to let that person go for my growth. Like the rocket boosters. Because I can't reminisce with anyone else on the planet about those things. He was there with me for all those things. Most people don't know 90% of what we went through and I can't have those conversations with anyone else because of that. So yes, it's hard. But was it worth it? One million percent. Because I have become the rocket ship that I was meant to be without those boosters.

But now, some of these people are slowing you down. And if you don't let them fall away, you're never going to reach the altitude you're capable of reaching.

And that's okay. It doesn't mean they're bad people. It doesn't mean you failed them. It just means your paths are diverging. And that's part of growth.

I had to let go of people when I moved to Florida. People I loved. People I'd known my whole life. But I knew that if I stayed connected to them, I was going to stay stuck. So I let them go. And it hurt. But it was necessary.

And if you're holding on to people who are draining your energy, who are doubting your vision, who are keeping you small, let them go. Wish them well. Be grateful for your time together. But let them fall away. Because your rocket is headed somewhere they're not meant to go.

One Uncomfortable Action This Week

Here's your first mental exercise for this chapter. I want you to do one thing this week that makes you uncomfortable. One thing that pushes you outside your comfort zone. One thing that scares you a little bit.

Maybe it's going to a networking event or signing up for one that's a couple of months from now. Maybe it's reaching out to someone you admire. Maybe it's spending money on something you've been hesitating to invest in. Maybe it's having a difficult conversation. Maybe it's applying for a job you don't think you're qualified for.

I don't care what it is. Just do something. Because inspired action always feels a little bit scary. And if you're not scared, you're probably not pushing hard enough.

"I'm Just Gonna Law of Attraction This Shit"

Here's your second mental exercise for this chapter. This is what I tell myself when I get to the point where I don't know what to do next or how I'm going to make it through. And literally 100% of the time since I started doing that, I have not only made it through, but I've made it through with better results than I had anticipated.

So the next time you're in a situation where you feel overwhelmed, where you feel out of place, where you feel like you don't know what to do, say this phrase to yourself: "I'm just gonna law of attraction this shit."

Say it out loud if you can. Or just say it in your head. And then let go. Trust the process. Trust that the universe put you in that situation for a reason. And trust that it's going to work out.

Because it will. It always does. As long as you show up and stay open.

Act Like You've Been There

Here's your third mental exercise for this chapter. The next time you walk into a room where you feel like you don't belong, practice this. Walk in with your head up. Make eye contact. Smile. Introduce yourself. Act like you've been there before.

Even if you haven't. Even if you're nervous. Even if your ego is screaming at you that you're an impostor.

Act like you belong. And watch how people respond. Watch how the energy shifts. Watch how opportunities start showing up just because you had the confidence to walk into the room.

The mental work is important. But it's not enough. You've got to take action. You've got to show up. You've got to put yourself in rooms where your manifestation can find you. Because the universe can only deliver what you're willing to receive. And if you're sitting at home waiting for it to show up, you're going to be waiting a long time. So get up. Get out. And watch what happens.

CHAPTER EIGHTEEN:
HOW BAD DO YOU WANT IT?
(AND WELCOME TO THE MOVEMENT)

Let me ask you a question. And I want you to really think about the answer...

How bad do you want it?

Not how bad do you say you want it. Not how bad you want it when you're feeling motivated. Not how bad you want it when things are going well.

How bad do you actually want it?

Because here's the truth. You get out exactly what you put in. No more. No less. And if you're not willing to put in the work—the real work, the uncomfortable work, the daily work—you're not going to get the results.

This isn't a game. This isn't something you try for a week and then quit when it doesn't instantly transform your life. This is a lifestyle. This is a commitment. This is something you do every single day for the rest of your life.

And the people who actually manifest what they want? They're the ones who answer that question with absolute certainty. "I want it bad enough to do whatever it takes."

40 Hours a Week for 17 Years

Let me tell you what I did. For 17 years, I dedicated 40 hours a week to this work. Not 40 hours at my job. 40 hours studying manifestation, the brain, consciousness, spirituality, psychology, neuroscience. Reading books. Watching documentaries. Conducting interviews. Testing mental exercises. Trying things. Failing. Adjusting. Trying again. I am a professional trier.

Forty hours a week. While everyone else was working their 9-to-5, I was working on my mind. While everyone else was coming home and watching TV, I was meditating, visualizing, running scenarios in Future Land.

I conducted over 2,000 interviews, live streamed. I read hundreds of books. I studied every teacher, every philosophy, every technique I could find. I took what worked and discarded what didn't. I combined methods. I created new exercises. I field-tested everything.

And that's why I can stand here today and tell you with absolute certainty that this works. Not because I got lucky. Not because I'm special. But because I put in the work. For 17 years. Forty hours a week.

So when someone tells me, "I tried affirmations for three days and nothing happened," I ask them the same question. How bad do you want it?

Because if you're not willing to put in more than three days, you don't want it badly enough. And if you don't want it bad enough, you're not going to get it.

The Friend Who Won't Lose Weight

Let me tell you about a friend of mine. He's been trying to lose weight for years. And I mean years. He's tried everything. Diets. Personal trainers. Hypnotherapy. Pills. Surgery. Everything.

Except for the one thing that would actually work. Changing his thoughts about food.

And every time I see him, he tells me about the new thing he's trying. The new diet. The new program. The new pill. And I listen. And I nod. And I let him talk.

And then I say, "When you're serious about losing weight, call me."

And he looks at me like I'm crazy. I'm doubting his resolve. And I am.

But I do understand. I lost 69 pounds without exercising once. I know exactly how hard it is. And I also know that it's not about the diet or the pills or the surgery. It's about the mental work. And until he's willing to do that work, nothing else is going to stick.

So I keep telling him the same thing. "When you're serious, call me."

Because I can't do the work for him. I can't force him to change his thoughts. I can only show him the path. And he has to decide if he's willing to walk it.

And that's the same question I'm asking you. Are you serious? Or are you just looking for the easy way out?

The 35 Alarms vs How Many You Actually Do

I told you earlier that I have 35 alarms on my phone. And that I probably only respond to 6 or 7 of them each day.

And you might be thinking, "Well, if you only do 6 or 7, why do you set 35?"

Because if I only set 6 or 7, I'd probably only do 2 or 3. And 2 or 3 isn't enough.

But when I set 35, I do 6 or 7. And 6 or 7 is enough to keep me awake. Enough to keep me focused. Enough to remind me what I'm working toward.

That's how bad I want it. I set 35 alarms knowing I'm only going to respond to a fraction of them. Because I'd rather aim high and hit a little lower than aim low and miss completely.

So the question is, how many alarms are you setting? Are you setting 35 and doing 6? Or are you setting 3 and doing none?

Because the number of alarms you're willing to set is a direct reflection of how bad you want it. And if you're not willing to set the alarms, you're not going to do the work. And if you're not willing to do the work, you're not going to get the results.

Most People Say "I'll Start Monday"

You know what I hear all the time? "I'll start Monday."
I'll start the mental exercises Monday.
I'll start visualizing Monday.
I'll start eating healthy Monday.
I'll start caring on Monday.
And Monday comes. And they say it again. "I'll start Monday."
And the cycle repeats. Over and over. Until they look up and realize they've been saying "I'll start Monday" for five years. And they're still in the exact same place they were five years ago.

And you know why? Because they don't want it badly enough.

If they wanted it badly enough, they wouldn't wait until Monday. They'd start today. Right now. This second.

Because watering seeds happens now. Not Monday. Now. And every day you wait, you're watering the wrong seeds. You've been watering seeds this whole time. You're reinforcing the life you're trying to escape instead of creating the life you're trying to build.

So stop saying "I'll start Monday." Start today. Start now. Because now is the only moment you ever have any power in. And if you keep giving that power away to some future version of Monday that never comes, you're never going to change.

You Don't Have to Tell Anyone

Here's something I want you to understand. You don't have to tell anyone about this book. You don't have to tell anyone you're doing mental exercises. You don't have to announce your manifestations on social media.

Just do the work. Quietly. Privately. Consistently.

And let your results speak for themselves.

Because here's what's going to happen. You're going to start manifesting things. Small things at first. Then bigger things. Then things that seem impossible. And people are going to notice.

They're going to ask you, "How did you do that? What's your secret?" And that's when you tell them. Not before. After.

Because when you tell people what you're doing before you have results, they doubt you. They judge you. They send you low-frequency energy. And that makes it harder to manifest.

But when you show them the results first, they can't argue. They can't doubt. They can't judge. Because the proof is right in front of them.

So be the example. Be the person in your family who breaks the cycle. Be the person in your office who levels up. Be the person in your friend group who achieves what everyone else thought was impossible.

And when they ask you how you did it, hand them this book. And welcome them to the movement.

Why I Do This (It's Not About the Money)

Let me tell you why I do this work. Because it's not about the money. I could make a lot more money doing something else. I could go back into law enforcement consulting. I could do private security work. I could do a hundred different things that would pay more than speaking at conferences and writing books.

But I don't do this for the money. I do this because I believe I'm here to change the world. The proof in my life has shown me repeatedly that this is what I'm meant to do.

I do this because I believe that if everyone on the planet changed just one more negative thought to positive each day, we'd reach a tipping point. We'd create a shift. We'd build a New Earth.

And that's not some pie-in-the-sky fantasy. That's a real possibility. Because collective consciousness is real. Collective energy is real. And when enough people raise their frequency, it raises the frequency of the entire planet.

That's what I'm working toward. That's what this book is about. That's what this movement is about.

It's not about helping you get rich. It's not about helping you get the car or the house or the relationship. I mean, yes, those things are great. And yes, this can help you manifest them. But that's not the end goal.

The end goal is to wake you up. To help you remember who you really are. To help you step into your power. To help you become the version of yourself that changes not just your own life, but the lives of everyone around you.

Because when you change, you change your family. When you change your family, you change your community. When you change your community, you change the world.

That's how this works. That's how we create a New Earth. One person at a time. One thought at a time. One manifestation at a time.

The Day I Stopped Working for Free

Let me tell you a story about why I finally learned my worth.

I've been working with professional athletes. I've coached NFL players to five Super Bowl victories.

Here's how it goes. I had a conversation with myself in a police car where I asked if I could sit at home, study the brain, and help mankind on a larger scale. This was the first real conversation I had with God. Growing up, when we prayed at night before bed, I just felt like I was talking at the wall, talking outward into the universe. This felt like my first one-on-one conversation with God. Like me and you sitting in a room talking to each other, and everyone else walking by is just background. A real engaged conversation.

I asked God: Let me sit at home, study the human brain, and help the world on a larger scale, not just the citizens of Camden City.

Like a voice, an intuitive voice that might tell you to duck if something was flying at you or turn left, I heard a voice say, "Okay. But whatever I show you, no matter how silly or crazy it may make you look, you have to show the world."

And just like any great news, I'd want to shout it from the mountaintops anyway, so I agreed.

Shortly after, I retired.

Nowhere in this pact was money mentioned.

So from 2008 until 2022, everything I did was basically volunteer. I accepted tips. But I worked volunteer. AAA, Triple A, college, high school, middle school, it didn't matter.

And no matter how many business coaches and all these other people that I interviewed over the years thought I was crazy and that I was devaluing myself, one person got the point through. And it was Elijah.

We were talking about one of my Eagles players who shouted me out on social media, and I was showing it to him. The guy was standing in front of a Lamborghini in front of a mansion.

Elijah knows me well. He'd been trying to get across to me for a while that I should charge for my services, just like all the other business coaches who told me I was crazy for not charging. He wasn't getting through.

But in this attempt, while showing him the social media post, he points to the Lamborghini and says, "Isn't that the car you want?"

And though it's not the same color or exact model, I shook my head. Yeah. I said, "Yeah."

And he said, "Isn't that the house you want?" And he pointed to the mansion in the background. And it wasn't the same mansion that I wanted, but I had no choice but to shake my head and say yeah. Because it looked like it. Big, white, beautiful.

And he said, "Well, that's what he got out of the Super Bowl. What did you get out of it? A social media shout-out?"

Though I had received a large tip for my services, what he said to me really drove home and pieced together every time someone had told me that.

When I charge nothing, when I charge zero, people see my value as zero. And I need to be compensated for the time I'm taking away from my children to travel and be on all these stages. Everything just made sense to me when he said that.

So I told him, I said, "Okay, go ahead, get me something. Get me a gig."

And that is when he got me my first real paying speaking gig for On Diem, Joe Fogg, in Nashville.

So Elijah was the one who convinced me to start charging for my services and be compensated for my time.

Fourteen years. From 2008 to 2022, everything I did was volunteer and I accepted tips.

I'm not saying if you're giving it away for free to stop. Of course you want to give for free. You want to donate some of your time. But you also want to be compensated for the time you're taking away from your family and the energy that you're spending on airplanes and all that other stuff.

You are valuable. Your time is valuable. Your expertise is valuable. And it's time you started acting like it.

New Jersey vs Florida Mentality

In my humble opinion, let me tell you the difference between living in New Jersey and living in Florida. And this is a generalization, but it's true enough to matter.

In New Jersey, if you figure out a way to make money, you keep it to yourself. You don't tell anyone. You don't share the blueprint. You hold it close because you're afraid someone's going to steal it from you.

In Florida, it's the opposite. If you figure out a way to make money, you share it. You tell everyone. You help people. You bring them along with you. Because there's an abundance mindset. There's a belief that there's enough for everyone.

And that's the mentality you need to have if you're going to manifest abundance. Not scarcity. Not competition. Not fear that someone's going to take what's yours.

Abundance. Generosity. Collaboration.

Because when you operate from abundance, you attract abundance. When you help other people succeed, you succeed. When you share what you know, you create a network of people who are rooting for you.

That's how I built my life in Florida. I shared everything. I helped everyone. And in return, I got more opportunities, more connections, and more success than I ever would have gotten if I'd kept everything to myself.

So stop hoarding. Stop gatekeeping. Stop acting like there's not enough to go around. Because there is. There's more than enough. And the more you give, the more you receive.

The "How Bad Do You Want It?" Audit

Here's your first mental exercise for this chapter. And this one's going to require some brutal honesty.

Go to the mirror. Sit down. And say out loud what you're willing to sacrifice to get what you want.

Not what you hope you'll sacrifice. Not what you think you should sacrifice. What are you actually willing to give up?

Are you willing to sacrifice Netflix time to do mental exercises? How many minutes a day?

Are you willing to sacrifice sleep to meditate at midnight?

Are you willing to sacrifice scrolling on your phone?

Are you willing to sacrifice comfort to go to networking events?

Are you willing to sacrifice toxic relationships to protect your energy?

Are you willing to sacrifice your ego to learn from people who know more than you?

Say it in the mirror. Say it out loud. Don't write it down. Say it. Because what you're willing to sacrifice is a direct reflection of how badly you want it.

And if you're not willing to sacrifice anything, you don't want it bad enough. And that's okay. But don't lie to yourself about it. Don't pretend you want it when you're not willing to do what it takes to get it.

The Alert Test

Here's your second mental exercise for this chapter. Set 10 alerts on your phone today. Right now. Before you move on to the next page.

Alerts, not alarms. Alerts are less invasive than alarms that just blare until you hit them or hit the snooze button. It needs to be an alert that just vibrates once so you can acknowledge it and move on.

Set them at random times throughout the day. Make them vibrate once with a message. "Check your thoughts." "I deserve this." "Thank you." Whatever message resonates with you.

And at the end of the day, count how many of those alerts you actually responded to. How many times you actually stopped and did a mental exercise.

That number is your current level of commitment. That number is how badly you currently want it.

And if that number is lower than you'd like, that's okay. But now you know. And now you can adjust. You can set more alerts. You can try harder. You can recommit.

Because the alerts don't lie. They show you exactly where you're at. And once you know where you're at, you can decide where you want to go.

90-Day Letter

Here's your third mental exercise for this chapter. This is one exercise I picked up along the way speaking with other mindset enthusiasts.

I want you to write a letter to yourself from the future. Specifically, from 90 days in the future.

Start the letter like this: "Dear [Your Name], you won't believe what I've done in the last 90 days..."

And then write everything you've manifested. Everything you've accomplished. Everything you've become. Write it as if it's already happened. As if it's already true. As if you're looking back on the last 90 days and marveling at how much your life has changed.

Be specific. Be detailed. Make it feel real.

And then fold that letter up. Put it somewhere safe. And 90 days from now, pull it out and read it. And see how much of it came true.

Because I promise you, if you do the work, if you stay committed, if you answer the question "How bad do you want it?" with your actions instead of your words, that letter is going to blow your mind.

The "Be the Example" Challenge

Here's your fourth mental exercise for this chapter. For the next 30 days, don't tell anyone what you're doing. Don't post about it on social media. Don't talk about your manifestations. Don't explain the Law of Attraction to anyone.

Just do the work. Quietly. Consistently. Every single day.

And let your results speak for themselves.

Because at the end of 30 days people are going to notice. They're going to see the change in you. They're going to see your energy shift. They're going to see things showing up in your life. And they're going to ask.

And when they ask, that's when you tell them. That's when you hand them this book. That's when you welcome them to the movement.

Daily Gratitude for Your ATM

Here's your fifth mental exercise for this chapter. Every single day, before you go to bed, I want you to say thank you to yourself.

Not to the universe. Not to God. To yourself.

Thank yourself for your ability to manifest. Thank yourself for the work you put in today. Thank yourself for setting the alerts. Thank yourself for doing the exercises. Thank yourself for staying committed.

Because you are the one doing this. You are the one creating your reality. You are the one putting in the work. And you deserve to be acknowledged for that.

So every night, look in the mirror and say, "Thank you. I'm proud of you. You're doing an amazing job."

And mean it. Because you are.

Your Ability to Manifest Is Everything

Let me be clear about something before we close this book. You can know all of this. You can read every chapter. You can understand every concept. You can memorize every mental exercise. But if you don't believe in your ability to manifest, you can say everything you want and even feel the emotions, and it just doesn't matter. It just doesn't matter.

You have to have faith in your ability to manifest. And you have to do the work and take inspired action.

Most great speakers and authors write a book where they touch on three to six subjects. But over and over they tell hundreds of stories from their life. But as you can see by the index of this book, there are dozens of subjects that need to be touched on.

If you really want to manifest to the best of your ability, this book aims to be a compilation of everything I've learned over the last 17 to 18 years. So instead of reading five books that touch on five points, you get 25. You got them all here.

So yes, it'll be tough, then it'll get annoying, but well worth it if you make it your mission. Watch the seeds that you water. Your life has now changed, this right here was about recruitment. You'll try this, it'll work, again and again… it's a law. Welcome, you are now part of the movement. Welcome.

— From "The Resume"

This is it. This is the moment when you decide. How bad do you want it? Are you willing to do the work? Are you willing to set the alerts, do the exercises, take the action, and stay committed even when it gets hard?

Because if you are, if you answer that question with absolute certainty, then nothing can stop you. Nothing.

You're going to manifest things you never thought possible. You're going to become the person you've always wanted to be. You're going to change your life. And you're going to change the lives of everyone around you.

And that's what this is all about. Not just changing your life. Changing the world. One person at a time. One thought at a time. One manifestation at a time.

Welcome to the movement.

Now go show them what you're capable of.

"THE RESUME"
A POEM BY NEO POSITIVITY

In the most dangerous city in America, a child was born to two parents and two sisters…

Raised by just his Dad since 1989, Puerto Rican and Black is his ethnic mixture.

Excelling in comedy, football, and karate, rarely ever being second best,

Becoming a cop in that town, and losing a sister, put him through some crazy test.

Since a young boy he was curious, about the brain, the answers to life and everything.

He saw a movie, called *"The Secret",* and like Red Bull, he grew wings.

Listening to every ounce of his being, which screamed to him, "that's your path",

He studied, and practiced, and studied some more, doing all the math.

Science + religion - everything that can be doubted, left him with a perfect system, every answer, unclouded.

No need for blind faith, no answers he should chase, he tried it, and it worked religiously. Soon all his troubles were erased.

The third law of motion demands that every action has an opposite and equal reaction,

Which means what you send out, will come back to you, some call that the Law of Attraction.

When you have a thought, it gets dispersed, across the entire universe, then it gets reversed, right back at you…

Then the world will do whatever it needs to, for the law of motion to maintain its statue---

-As a law, if you hate or don't appreciate, that trend, in your life, will continue.

If what you've been doing doesn't have you excelling, then you should look into a different venue.

In order for change, you must change, but you gotta know how, knowledge is not only power, it's the key.

What have you been focusing on? Between proactively thinking, life's a garden and you've been watering seeds.

And when they bloom, don't be surprised if what's in front of your eyes is the same thing you see daily...or worse.

Negativity breeds negative outcomes, positive thoughts breed positive outcomes,

"thoughts become things" can be a gift or a curse.

Like the time he was worried that his car would break down and it did, the law of motion struck again.

Or the times he was worried that the ones who he trusted, weren't being such good friends.

Or the millions of times he meditated, on the good life, where he never had to work again,

And now that's the life that he lives, because he watered that seed, despite the fact he was broke with no end in sight.

Listen carefully to what I said, times were tough, he should have been sad, mad or furious with a chest full of pain,

But he'd learned that if he let the negative thoughts play out, he'd only be manifesting those same things.

So when the chips were down, he was up! When life told him he was stuck, he screamed, "NO, I'm in control of my thoughts."

"And since thoughts become things, I have all control. That makes sense, but that's not what I've been taught."

Every second of each and every day of your lives, these rules, much like gravity, are inescapably followed.

He always says, "show me your predominant thoughts and I'll show you your tomorrow."

But controlling one's thought is the hardest occupation a man can have according to both science and religion,

So yea, it'll be tough, then it'll get annoying, but well worth it if you make it your mission.

Now imagine a world, where everyone heard this, and changed just one more negative thought to positive each day,

Their positivity would spread, we know how good vibes work, + the seeds that they watered would be on their way.

The rich keep getting richer, the poor keep getting poorer, fear is one thing that can make people change.

When a negative thought creeps in, "END IT!", play it out with YOUR ending, know the outcome, and remember life's game.

Watch the seeds that you water. Your life has now changed. This, right here, is about recruitment.

You'll try this and it'll work, again and again…**it's a law**.

Welcome, You are now part of the movement.
Welcome.